THE DALTON BROTHERS

The Jingle Bob Press was established more than twenty years ago by James D. Horan, novelist and historian, and his wife, Gertrude, with the goal of eventually reprinting many of the rare books on the Wild West from their collection.

The Jingle Bob imprint is derived from the brand used by John Chisum, the cattle king of New Mexico. The brand was known as Jingle Bob because of Chisum's practice of splitting the steer's ear, causing the lower part to hang loosely. Also called "Long Rail" or "Fence Rail," the brand was used by Chisum during the period of the Lincoln County War in the 1870s and was kept up by his heirs until 1894.

Curiously, photographs or sketches of the brand are rare. This one is reproduced by courtesy of V. C. Roybal, Reference Librarian, New Mexico Highlands University, Las Vegas, New Mexico.

To maintain the flavor of the rare Western classics reprinted in this series, the original versions have been reprinted without change, including any original misprints or errors in spelling or grammar.

THE JINGLE BOB BRAND

THE DALTON BROTHERS

AND THEIR

ASTOUNDING CAREER OF CRIME

BY

AN EYE WITNESS

With numerous illustrations reproduced from photographs
taken on the spot

The Pinkerton Detective Series. Quarterly. $1.00 Annually.
No. 6 Dec. 1892. Entered at Chicago Post
Office as second-class matter.

CHICAGO
LAIRD & LEE, Publishers

With an Introduction by James D. Horan

JINGLE BOB/CROWN PUBLISHERS, INC.
NEW YORK

Library of Congress Cataloging in Publication Data

[Valcourt-Vermont, Edgar de]
  The Dalton brothers and their astounding career of crime.

  1. Dalton family.   2. Outlaws—The West.   3. Outlaws—The West—
Biography.   4. The West—Biography.   I. An eye witness.   II. Title.
F595.D15V34 1977   364.1′55′0922 [B]   77-4435
ISBN 0-517-53108-9

CONTENTS.

PART THE FIRST.

CRIMINAL BOYS.

CHAPTER I.

CHAPTER V. PAGE

CHAPTER VI.

PART THE THIRD.

DEAD CRIMINALS.

CHAPTER I.

CHAPTER II.

CHAPTER III. PAGE

CHAPTER IV.

CHAPTER V.

CHAPTER VI.

INTRODUCTION
WHEN THE DALTONS RODE
By James D. Horan

The Dalton band of outlaws was the last blood brotherhood in the history of Western outlawry. In the final days of a fading frontier they staged their celebrated raid on Coffeyville, Kansas, in an attempt to outdo the exploits of Jesse James by robbing two banks at the same time.

However, outraged citizens, not impressed by the gang's lurid publicity, reached for their six-shooters and rifles and fought a bloody battle with the bank and train robbers. When the last shot had been fired, only one member of the brotherhood had survived and four townsmen were dead.

It was the second time that ordinary citizens, without the help of sheriffs, marshals, or posses, had refused to be intimidated by the reputation of a Western robber band. The first time was in 1876 at Northfield, Minnesota, when the James-Younger gang was shattered. After that, Jesse James reorganized a pale imitation of his band, only to become the most hunted man in the nation until a youthful Bob Ford killed him in the living room of his home in St. Joseph, Missouri. Jesse had been living there with his family while he planned what he told Bob Ford and his brother, Charlie, would be "the biggest exploit of my life," the robbery of the Platte City bank.[1]

In Coffeyville, citizen guns blasted the Daltons into history. Only Emmett, the youngest, survived. He lived on into the twentieth century and became a building contractor in Los Angeles. He died in 1937. One of the first books written about the gang was *The Dalton Brothers and Their Astounding Career of Crime*, by "An Eye Witness," published in yellow paperback covers by Laird & Lee, Chicago, 1892. The author has never been identified but was probably a Chicago or Kansas newspaperman. The book is a classic of Western outlawry, beloved by collectors.[2]

Unlike a large number of nineteenth-century paperbacks written about outlaws, "Eye Witness" appears to have carefully researched the history of the Daltons and interviewed eyewitnesses to the Coffeyville disaster and train robberies committed by the gang.

It is evident that the author obtained a great deal of material from U.S. Deputy Marshal Ransom Payne, who chased the gang but never caught up with them—with the exception of the train robbery at the small Wharton depot in the Cherokee Strip, when the Daltons held up Train No. 403, the fast Texas Express. This time gold was secondary: the gang was looking for Payne, who was on the train.

---

[1] James D. Horan, *Desperate Men* (revised) (New York: 1962), pp. 117–47; William A. Settle, Jr., *Jesse James Was His Name* (Columbia, Missouri: 1966), pp. 92–97; Homer Croy, *Jesse James Was My Neighbor* (New York: 1949), pp. 245, 280.

[2] Ramon Adams, in his *Six Guns and Saddle Leather* (Norman, Oklahoma: 1954), describes the book as "scarce, correct in most details."

The marshal, sleeping in the last car, was awakened by shots and the wild cries of the bandits as they surrounded the engine. He dove into the bushes alongside the tracks and, gun in hand, waited until the outlaws, at last believing the conductor's story that Payne had missed connections, robbed the express safe of sixteen hundred dollars and rode off.

"Eye Witness" paid off Payne with elaborate praise. The marshal is described as "a fearless enemy of evil-doers," "a shrewd discoverer of apparently lost trails," and "skilled," "indefatigable," "intrepid," and so on.

Twenty-five years ago over dinner, an old friend, Burton Rascoe, editor, literary columnist, and author of a biography of Belle Starr, called Payne an egotist, a frontier fraud who tried to steal credit for dangerous tasks done by other, more competent law officers.[3]

Harold Preece, author of *The Dalton Gang: End of an Outlaw Era*, at a later time told me that he had the same opinion of Payne.

I disagree with both men. In his interview with "Eye Witness" Payne did not exaggerate the role he had played in the saga of the Daltons; he simply recited what he knew, firsthand.

He described, for instance, the night he was forced to hide in the grass along the tracks while the Daltons searched the railroad cars for him. Rascoe insisted this was a cowardly act. However, newspaper accounts reported that there were on board an estimated fifty passengers, many of them undoubtedly armed, yet not one fired a shot or tried to form a group to resist. It would have been senseless for the outnumbered Payne single-handedly to engage the gang.

Payne also described how he once trailed the Daltons to one of their hideouts only to find that they had fled. He did not try to put himself in Coffeyville at the time of the raid but told "Eye Witness" that he was one of the first law officers on the scene and obtained a statement from Emmett Dalton. (The first was probably Chris Madsen, who with the renowned Bill Tilghman later broke up the Doolin gang.)

In a time when it was not unusual for lawmen to be cowards or corrupt—Henry (Hendry) Brown, who had ridden with Billy the Kid and became sheriff of Caldwell, Kansas, was killed after he tried to rob the bank of neighboring Medicine Lodge—Payne's record as a U.S. Deputy Marshal is impressive. He solved at least two killings in the new Oklahoma Territory and delivered the murderers to the federal penitentiary where they had been sentenced to a life term.[4]

Payne can't be blamed for the author's occasionally florid prose, and it is doubtful that he used any of the dialogue attributed to him.

Payne also gave "Eye Witness" a fascinating insight into the duties and pay of a frontier deputy marshal. His salary was two dollars for

[3] Burton Rascoe, *Belle Starr: The Bandit Queen* (New York: 1941), p. 310.

[4] William Keleher, *Violence in Lincoln County* (Albuquerque, New Mexico: 1957), pp. 324–25; James D. Horan, *The Authentic Wild West: The Gunfighters* (New York: 1976), p. 50.

making an arrest and six cents a mile for travel expenses. He had to have his bill approved by Washington, and only when the bureaucrats were ready did he receive his check. After cashing it he had to give the marshal 25 percent, which was the marshal's legal commission. However, it wasn't a bad life: passenger rates were two cents a mile, a good meal and lodging could be had for fifty cents, and a 150-mile journey from Fort Smith to bring back a prisoner could result in a twelve-dollar paycheck, even after the marshal's commission had been deducted. The deputy could also add to his income by serving government subpoenas, and he was permitted to accept reward money offered by express companies, counties, states, and the American Bankers Association.

When a bank or train robber was killed, the deputy would tie the corpse to a board, prop it up against an outside wall, and summon the local photographer. The picture would be sent to the Chicago office of Pinkerton's National Detective Agency, where the dead man's photo and description would be compared with Bertillion charts, a primitive national rogues' gallery. If the charts matched the dead man, the Pinkertons would forward any existing reward to the deputy.[5]

Some of the writing of "Eye Witness" is typical nineteenth-century pulp. A good example is his opening scene of the Dalton family, in which he has the mother of the clan saying to herself:

"Where are they all, I wonder . . . 'Tain't fair to leave an old rheumatic thing like me, and a flighty wench like Minnie, to take care of a house and a sick boy, too. Ah, my! life's harder than it ought to be, by a great deal—"

However, despite his fictionalized dialogue, "Eye Witness" gives a solid account of train robberies and the trailing of the gang by lawmen. Rascoe was contemptuous of Payne because in two years he never arrested a member of the band. However, it is important to keep in mind the vast distances he would have had to cover, the Daltons' many kinfolk and sympathizers who hid them, and the very small number of law officers assigned to the frontier by a budget-conscious Washington.

In contrast with Payne's efforts and deeds was the established fact that local state, federal officers and the Pinkertons never knew what Jesse James looked like for the fifteen years they hunted him.

The account of the Coffeyville raid by "Eye Witness" is excellent, rivaling the one written by David Stewart Elliott, publisher and editor of the *Coffeyville Journal*, who took part in the fight and wrote his account immediately after the battle.[6]

"Eye Witness" presents excerpts from Emmett Dalton's confession, obtained by Marshal Payne. In it Dalton supplies the motivation for the foolhardy raid: "Bob said he would discount the James boys and rob both banks in Coffeyville at the same time." Evidently Bob Dalton,

[5] James D. Horan, *The Pinkertons: The Detective Dynasty That Made History* (New York: 1967), pp. 363–64.

[6] David Stewart Elliott, *Last Raid of the Daltons. A reliable account of the battle with the bandits at Coffeyville, Kansas, October 5, 1892.* First Edition illustrated by E. A. Filleau (Coffeyville, Kansas: *Coffeyville Journal* print, 1892).

the gang's leader, had come to believe his press clippings.

An excellent street map showing where the action took place is also included, along with sketches—one depicting the badly wounded Emmett Dalton in bed in the Farmer's Home, a small boarding house in Coffeyville. On the jacket is an engraving of the dignified, mustachioed Marshal Payne, described as "the marshal who kept on the trail of the Dalton Gang for over Two Years."

The book by "Eye Witness" is a classic of Western Americana and very scarce.

BIBLIOGRAPHY

BOOKS

Adams, Ramon. *Six Guns and Saddle Leather*. Norman, Oklahoma: 1954.

Croy, Homer. *He Hanged Them High*. New York: 1952.

———. *Trigger Marshal*. New York: 1958.

Dalton, Emmett (with Jack Jungmeyer). *When the Daltons Rode*. New York: 1937.

Elliott, David Stewart. *Last Raid of the Daltons*. Coffeyville, Kansas: 1892.

Harlow, Alvin. *Old Waybills*. New York: 1934.

Harman, S. W. *Hell on the Border*. Chicago: 1898.

Harrington, Fred Harvey. *Hanging Judge*. Caldwell, Idaho: 1951.

Horan, James D. *Desperate Women*. New York: 1952.

Hunter, J. Marvin, and Rose, Noah H. *The Album of Gunfighters*. Bandera, Texas: 1951.

James, Marquis. *They Had Their Hour*. Indianapolis: 1934.

Masterson, Vincent. *The Katy Railroad and the Last Frontier*. Norman, Oklahoma: 1952.

Nix, Everitt Dumas. *Oklahombres*. St. Louis: 1929.

Preece, Harold. *Living Pioneers*. New York: 1952.

———. *The Dalton Gang: End of an Outlaw Era*. New York: 1963.

Raine, William MacLeod. *Famous Sheriffs and Western Outlaws*. New York: 1931.

Rascoe, Burton. *Belle Starr: Bandit Queen*. New York: 1931.

Shirley, Glenn. *Law West of Fort Smith*. New York: 1957.

———. *Six Gun and Silver Star*. New York: 1955.

Tilghman, Zoe. *Outlaw Days*. Oklahoma City: 1926.

———. *Marshal of the Last Frontier*. Glendale, California: 1949.

Wellman, Paul A. *A Dynasty of Western Outlaws*. New York: 1961.

NEWSPAPERS

The *Fort Smith Elevator* of 1890–1892 is an excellent source for accounts of the robberies committed by the Daltons and the activities of the lawmen who trailed them. See also newspapers of Oklahoma during the same period, particularly the *Crescent City Courier*, covering Logan County, and the *Quill*, a Shawnee weekly.

THE DALTON BROTHERS
And Their Astounding Career of Crime

PART THE FIRST

CRIMINAL BOYS

CHAPTER I.

A STRANGE NIGHT'S WORK—UNDERTAKER LANG'S GHASTLY
VISITORS—THE DALTONS' COVERED WAGON AND ITS
SILENT OCCUPANT—SHOT IN THE BACK AND
DISHONORED BY HIS MURDERERS.

A dark, dreary night in December, 1888.

On the open plains of Southern Kansas, the wind blows a hurricane of snow. The roads disappear under the white covering, and the city of Coffeyville, in Montgomery county, Kansas, just three miles from the Indian Territory limits, sleeps the sleep of the just.

It is a prosperous, strictly law-abiding community, populated with bright, active, sociable people who are proud of their promising town and

of the good days ahead for it and for them. The spires of numerous churches rise, here and there, as material evidence of the people's culture and religious feelings, while, in the business part of the city, several blocks of substantially-constructed brick buildings are clustered in sign of business activity. Indeed, Coffeyville is a worthy representative of that indomitable American spirit which has made the West a joy for the eyes and the hearts of men.

But to-night, the inhabitants have all withdrawn to their cosy homes, and doubtless enjoy the sweets of well-earned repose. It's almost one o'clock already, and hardly a light is visible inside the closed houses.

Suddenly the dull rumbling of a covered wagon is heard at a distance. It is rolling from the western direction, and the driver on the front seat is talking with some one seated behind him.

"Are you sure you know where he lives?" he asks, in evident ill-humor.

"Just half a block ahead, on Ninth street, I tell you; a two-story house with a brick basement, on the next corner to the right," is the precise answer given in a tone of command.

The driver grumbles something unintelligible, then shuts his lips tight, as if to keep the icy air out. At the place designated he stops his horse in front of a comfortable looking dwelling. Strange to say, there is a light burning on the upper floor; a sick one is perhaps keeping the mother awake. Anyhow, this sign of life brings out a satisfactory grunt on the driver's part:

"They won't keep us waiting long in that ——— of a weather," he swears. Then he begins calling out in a stentorian voice:

"Lang! Oh! Lang!"

At the second or third appeal, a window on the second floor is slightly lifted and a bearded man's face leans over, while a muffled voice answers:

"What are you after, you fellows, waking up a man in the dead of night?"

"It's a job for you we are after, Mr. Lang?" is the cool retort.

"Who are you, anyhow?"

"The Dalton Brothers from the territory, with a little parcel in this wagon to be delivered you C. O. D. Do you catch on?"

" s that you, Bob Dalton?" the householder queries.

"Bob it is; and Emmet's behind me with a silent customer he wants to introduce to you, Mr. Lang. Are you coming down? It's mighty cold here I tell you. Will drive you to the store."

"Is it a cash on the nail business?" queries the Coffeyville citizen, in a cautious way.

'Oh! it's all right. It's court money and it can't fail you, this month or next. A job on the square, I tell you. By G——, won't you hurry up? We'll be soon as stiff as our friend back there, if you don't hustle ——"

"I am coming, I am coming ——" is the welcome answer, and the window closes with a bang.

Five minutes later, the two occupants of the wagon are increased by one, not counting the strange freight they have been lugging around so mysteriously.

The horse's head is turned toward the business portion of the village—*city*, they like to call it, over there—and the party soon reaches the large store of

LANG & LAPE,

Furniture Dealers and Undertakers,

on Walnut street, three or four doors south of Eighth street.

They all alight, throw a blanket over the perspiring horse, and, while Mr. Lang fumbles with his key in the lock of the store-door, the two Daltons, tall, stalwart young men, lads rather, hardly out of their teens, walk to the back of the wagon and begin to unload its gruesome freight.

As the reader has doubtless surmised already. it is a corpse which has been the silent companior of the brothers during their midnight ride.   It is a powerfully heavy corpse, too, and the moonlight, just emerging from behind the clouds, shines over the features of a man of thirty or thereabout, with heavy moustache and clotted hair.

No sign of a bloody encounter is visible at the first glance; but as Bob Dalton turns the body on one side to take a better hold of the man's shoulders, a round, bullet-shaped hole, on the nape of the neck, reveals itself and tells its fearful story.   The man has been shot dead from behind—there has been murder here; revolting, cowardly murder.

With a composure far above their years, however, the two lads pursue their dread task and carry across the sidewalk, under the wide, wooden awning that extends all along this side of the street, the remains of the murdered man.   They soon lie in the

back part of the vast Lang & Lape store, and the proprietor examines them with his usual professional keenness.

He is not long before noticing the mortal wound behind the neck, and without saying a word he looks up toward the brothers, with a precise interrogation in his eyes.

"Know that man?" says Bob, the older one of the couple, answering a question by a question, as if to delay the coming revelation.

"No; never saw him before," is the curt, business-like reply.

"Name of party: Charles Montgomery."

"Well?"

Throwing back the lapel of his heavy overcoat, Bob now displays a U. S. Deputy Marshal's badge.

"Caught him in the act, three hours ago, burglar-izing Ted Seymour's stable, close to to the Kansas line."

"But that's in the territory limits, ain't it?"

"Yep."

"A short mile from your father's place?"

"Yep."

"How did you happen to be round that way, to-night?"

"Have had our suspicions, for quite a while; man was no good, anyhow; used to peddle whisky for the Indians, got sentenced a couple of times. A horse-thief besides."

"How do you know that ?"

"We know it, that's all. None of your business, Mister. We are officers of the law and are responsible to the courts only."

"That's all right. But I ain't going to bury a man that's come to his death through a gunshot in the back of his neck, before knowing a thing or two about the whole story. Kind of queer, don't you know ?"

It took no little courage for that unarmed citizen, all alone in his store, in this part of the city left absolutely unoccupied and unguarded, during the night, to thus boldly resist the entreaties,—the orders we might say,—of these two strapping chaps, armed to the teeth and evidently resolved to have their way at any cost. But cool presence of mind has tamed wilder characters than these, and Mr. Lang's interrogatories were finally answered with some sort of impatient respect.

The story, true or not, was simple enough. The brothers had lately enlisted in a regular mars'..'

posse in the territory; the elder one Bob, just twenty-one years old, had even been entrusted lately with a U. S. Deputy Marshal's badge, and so far, nothing had been said or whispered that could be held as detrimental to the boys' characters

Now, a few weeks before that eventful night, a tall, lanky Kentuckian had presented himself at a neighboring cattle range, asking for employment. He looked strong and willing enough, and the "boss" being in need of some extra hands gave him a "job" on the spot. He did his work satisfactorily and was soon "one of the boys."

It was not long, however, before—always according to Bob Dalton's narrative—queer stories were set afloat concerning the newcomer. He soon admitted, with a great show of frankness, that he had been engaged in Indian whisky trading, or rather smuggling, and had been "caught at it" a few times and been carried off to Fort Smith jail. But misdemeanors of that kind are so common round about the region that it hardly—if at all—lowered Charley Montgomery in his new associates' estimation.

The U. S. Deputy Marshals round about suspected him, however, of having been connected with various horse-stealings until then unpunished, and

felt sure that he would one day or other get tired of earning a scant, but honest, living and drop back into the easier—if more dangerous—avocation he had once adorned. So a quiet watch was kept over the man, and the Daltons, on a visit to their father's farm, had given a good deal of their time spying upon his every movement.

That very night, they declared, they had found him, a crowbar in his hands, attempting to unhinge the heavy door that led into Ted Seymour's, the rich cattle man's, stable. There were half a dozen fast sprinters located within the premises, and anyone of them would have been a valuable catch.

According to the unwritten law of the land, a man engaged in horse-stealing was entitled to a bullet or two in the body, before even a word of warning. And this the poor wretch had got with a vengeance.

"It has all been done on the square, Mister," Bob said, finishing his terse recital. "You'll have to take charge of him, you see; and we'll make our report to the Marshal and have the court at its next sitting allow you for your trouble and expenses. That's all there's about it. My brother and I are off to Fort Smith by first train, and we have to get the thing off your hands, see?"

2

The undertaker thought a while, and then carrying the only lamp, smoky and begrimed, that lighted up this weird scene, to a desk in the front part of the store, he sat down and silently indicted the following document:

"Delivered to Lang & Lape, undertakers of Coffeyville, Kansas, for burial, the body of one Charley Montgomery, who was caught by us last night, December —, 1888, burglarizing Ted Seymour's stable, and was shot by us while committing a crime.

"Expenses to be paid by the Marshal's office of the Indian Territory."

"Coffeyville, Kansas,—December, 1888."

"And you sign here, both of you," Mr. Lang added, having read aloud the contents of this declaration.

Without an instant's hesitation the young men put their hands to the pen and signed boldly:

"ROBERT DALTON, U. S. Deputy Marshal."

"EMMET DALTON."

"That'll do," the undertaker said; "I don't like that job half too much, but I'll have to do it and that's the end of it. Good-night, boys."

And the three men moved toward the door.

When they had reached the sidewalk and the undertaker had closed the door of his store, Bob said, with a show of cordiality:

"Want a lift to your house, Mr. Lang?"

"Never mind about that, Dalton; it's only a couple of blocks and I have just as lief walk home."

"All right!" was the elder boy's cool answer.

"Now, Em, you get it on the quick; we'll have to catch that 5:00 A. M. train on the Mo. Pac. So let her go."

The two lads were now seated in the wagon and Emmet was gathering the horse's reins.

"A nice, tight little place, this is," cried Bob, looking around approvingly. "You'll see us again, soon. Ta-ta!"

And the wagon rolled noiselessly away upon the snow-carpeted highway.

CHAPTER II.

———

"Ma! Ma!" a young, not unpleasant voice called out from inside a shabby, unpainted one-story farm building, a short distance away from the dusty road. Near the primitive well close by, a rougher voice answered:

"What's that you want, Minnie? 's Si complaining?"

"That he is, ma. Ain't the doctor a-coming soon?"

"Pa's gone for him these two hours. He won't be long now, I guess. Keep the boy under his blankets."

"I'm trying to, ma, but the child is that fretful that I don't know what to do with him."

"Well, tell him I'm coming soon. I'll make him some lemonade, directly."

And the old woman—she looked older and more bent, whiter of hair and more wrinkled, than her years warranted—pulled up the bucket full of fresh, sparkling water, and poured its contents into the pail by her side.

"Where are they all, I wonder," she soliloquized, moodily, "'tain't fair to leave an old rheumatic thing like me, and a flighty wench like Minnie, to take care of a house and a sick boy, too. Ah, my! life's harder than it ought to be, by a great deal.—" And heaving a deep sigh, the farmer-wife wended her tired steps toward her homely abode.

Just then she noticed a heavy cloud of dust upon the road leading east toward Coffeyville, the center portion of which could be easily espied at a few miles' distance.

"The doctor, I reckon," she muttered; "it's about time for him and pa to be here. I hope he won't be in a hurry for his pay, for if there is a half a dollar in this whole blessed shanty I'd like to see it.—"

The rhythmical tramp of numerous horses' hoofs soon informed the old woman that her surmises had been wrong. A troop of horsemen were coming up at a rapid trot in the direction of the house. It took her but a few seconds to recognize the new comers.

"Them's my boys!" she cried, with a look of motherly pride lighting up her furrowed features; and in her joy and evident relief, she cried out toward the open window of the house:

"Minnie! the boys, the boys!"

A blushing young face looked out, beaming with delighted surprise. It was easy enough to notice that there was something more than sisterly love in the radiance of the handsome blue eyes. So we might just as well inform the reader right here that Minnie Johnson was the niece, and not the daughter, of old Mrs. Louis Dalton, the old lady we have just seen at the farm well, the mother of the strapping young men and lads known and spoken of, not un- favorably at the time, as the *Dalton Boys.*

For this chapter opens in the late days of the fall of 1888, just six months before this momentous 22d of April, that threw open to the covetous greed of 60,000 settlers the rich plains of the Oklahoma region.

Shortly before that time, a family of eight people had come over from the Indian Territory to take up and rent a small farm in the immediate vicinity of Coffeyville, Kansas, quite close to the tracks of the Missouri Pacific R. R. company. The father was a

gloomy-looking, dull and morose individual, over sixty-five years old; his name was Louis Dalton, and his Irish origin could be easily guessed at from the fact of his having named two of his sons after those great Hibernian patriots, Grattan and Emmet.

The family seemed to have known better days, and the old people openly manifested their discontent at their reduced circumstances by having nothing but gruff and graceless speeches to address to outsiders or even to their own folks. Their unsociable ways cooled off any hospitable intentions on the part of their new neighbors, and it wouldn't have been long before complete isolation would have surrounded the humble Dalton establishment, had not the young people on the farm made up, plentifully, by their hearty way and hale-fellow-well-met demeanor, for the older ones' taciturn and ill-tempered manners.

Mother Dalton belonged to the famed—ill-famed rather—James and Younger families, being herself a half sister of the Younger brothers' father; she had been blessed with a large brood of children, fifteen in number—ten sons and five daughters. The veracious relator of this narration has only been able to trace the existence of seven among those boys and

of one of the girls. The latter married a butcher in good circumstances called Whipple, now located at Kingfisher, Oklahoma Territory, and of whom anon.

Of the seven boys above mentioned, all alive at the time, Ben, the elder, was his father's mainstay on the little farm by Coffeyville. He had reached already the respectable age of thirty-seven. Next to him a full-bearded, honest and energetic fellow, Frank by name, counted among the best deputies of the Arkansas U. S. Marshal; he was thirty or thereabout. Next to him Grattan, twenty-five, William, twenty-three, Robert, twenty-one, and Emmet, eighteen, were more generally known as *Grat, Bill, Bob* and *Em*, appellations they were soon to render criminally notorious all over this vast continent, although to Bob, Grat and Em, belong more especially the palm in this competition of evildoing. Simon, the fourteen year old lad, now lying upon a bed of sickness, closed this list of pillars of the *House of Dalton.*

Of the four boys old enough to be of help to their family or to fight for themselves in the struggle for life, Bob had been recently appointed one of the Deputy U. S. Marshals on duty in the Indian Terri-

tory, but reporting to the U. S. Marshal for the State
of Arkansas, with residence at Fort Smith.

His young brother, Emmet, who had always been
his particular chum and favorite, joined him in his
roving excursions through those sparsely-inhabited
regions; and Grat and Will fell in with them occasionally, although the latter preferred the Pacific coast
as his habitual abode. As a regular business, the two
elder boys tried mining, cattle driving, horse buying
and selling; anything and everything except the
dull but steady occupations, found on a farm or in
city life. They were all fond of a free, untrammeled
existence, on horseback mostly, with plain but sub-
stantial clothing on their back, the rough fare they
could find on the road, and the few rather riotous
pleasures of an occasional tear-out.

Perhaps had they inherited from their mother,
who has been said to have Indian as well as outlaw's
blood in her veins, that hankering for a roaming,
open-air life, full of exciting variety and which
might or might not, according to circumstances,
carry them over to a career of open defiance of
human law. Whatever may be the case, they had
managed so far to remain within the bounds of
comparative respectability, and their popularity in

those rural districts, and even in the small cities that dot this vast region, had been growing month after month.

No untoward incident had embittered those young, primitive hearts and filled them with a dangerous desire after vengeance under some form or other.

It was not to be long though before just such an incident would throw three of these healthy, energetic and promising youths out of the straight road and turn their destiny into the disastrous and guilty channel, the goal of which was to be ——Death.

As is almost invariably the case, this incident was to have its origin in love, love thwarted, love betrayed, revengeful and merciless Love!

And the culminating point of this dramatic adventure was to be reached within a few short weeks from the day we see the four happy horsemen ride, merrily singing a rollicking refrain, into the farmyard of old man Louis Dalton.

"Hello! Minnie!" cried Bob, who had been scanning the front of the house with marked attention.

"Hello! Bob!" was the joyful reply, while the young girl waved her hand in token of welcome.

The four men jumped out of the saddle and led

their steeds to the rough hewn trough by the well. One of them set himself a-pumping, whistling "Home, Sweet Home," with all his might, while the horses were being relieved of saddle, bags and blankets

"Where is Si?" queried Grat, who had a kind of protective feeling toward the little chap, never in the best of health; the only *puny* one of the family.

We forgot to say that each son had dutifully kissed old mother Dalton with the sincere marks of fond affection that sat well on their bronzed faces.

"In the back room there, in bed," answered the dame, resuming her whining tone which she had left aside for a while to welcome her visiting offspring.

"Poor little chap," said Grat; "is it so bad as that with him?"

"Yes it is; and your daddy has just been out after the doctor."

"Dr. Wood, you mean?" asked Bob, who had finished his task and was washing his head and hands previous to entering in the presence of his well-liked cousin.

"Yes, Dr. Wood; he is a good old man, and won't ask for his money right away, as some of them leeches do."

"Never mind the money, mother," cried Grat,

patting his pocket that gave forth a silvery sound. "We boys can stand a couple of doctors apiece if that's to make little Si well and hearty."

Just then a noise of wheels called every one's attention toward the road. Dr. J. A. Wood's buggy, with two persons aboard, was just stopping in front of the house.

The pleasant-featured old physician, with his long gray beard and his kindly smile, had soon joined the group around the well.

After a general handshaking, somebody noticed that "daddy had not come along."

"Oh! he is as perky as ever," cried Mother Dalton, querulously. "I guess he don't care a penny about any of you, boys. I am sometimes weeks without getting a word out of him. I say, leave him alone. If he can stand being cross, so can we; isn't that so, boys?"

A rather unanimous grunt ratified this somewhat unwifely sentiment, and not bothering any more about the head of the family, the whole party adjourned inside the house, the doctor and the mother taking the lead.

They all entered the scantily furnished living room which, with two small rooms on each side and

a kitchen in the rear, constituted the whole establishment. The door of one of the rooms was wide
open, and the excited cries of a small boy were
heard within. It called out:

"Grat, Grat, come to me quick!"

With something like a lump in his throat, the
tallest and oldest of the four brothers present walked,
first toward his little favorite's pallet, and leaning
over kissed the emaciated cheek of the feverish
child.

"Well, well," he said, mastering his emotion.
"What's matter with you, old fellow? I thought I'd
find you hopping around the farm happy as a lark."

The little hands pressed the bulky palm of the
big brother, while the boy, gasping for breath, said
in a voice exhausted by his recent exertions:

"Glad to see you, Gratty. Oh! so glad," and the
little fellow broke down, sobbing as if his heart
would break.

The good doctor was soon by the bedside, with
those soothing and encouraging words that are
worth "gallons of choice medicines."

"Never mind, my child; you'll be soon about again;
there's nothing much the matter with you, I'll bet.
Now, if you, big fellows, will kindly give the boy a

little fresh air and leave him to me and mother for a while, we'll see to it that he is up and going in a jiffy."

And with a wave of his hand, Dr. Wood had soon cleared a space around the bed and gradually taken possession of the room.   He closed the door behind the last of the visitors, and the mother aiding, began a thorough examination of the wee patient's ailment.

It didn't take him long to discover that the lad had been growing too fast, and was consequently suffering from a general debility, made much worse by the coarse food that was the only nourishment available. Having placed back the little sufferer upon its pillow of rough and not extra clean linen, he stepped out into the sitting-room and said:

"Boys, I guess you'll prove better doctors than I for the little chap. He is somewhat weak from over-growing and he'll have to get, for a while, some better food than cornbread and fried pork. So if you chip in something for to get him a better fare, beefsteaks and chickens, and lots of good eggs, I'll promise that he'll be another boy within a month."

The words were hardly out of the physician's mouth before every son of them had his hand in his pocket and had drawn it out full of coin.

"'Here you are, doc," cried Grat, acting the spokesman; for was not his little chum's life at stake? "You take the pile and buy what's needed. Mother might think it money thrown away. Just have the people at the store send what's needed, and if you want any more just let us know. We have been trading profitably of late, and we can't afford to have little Si die from want of proper food."

"Well said, Grat!" cried a cheery voice. The door of the other room had just been thrown open, and Minnie Johnson, arrayed in her best Sunday clothes, stood there beaming with honest affection, and applauding with both hands in sign of delighted welcome.

CHAPTER III.

MAKING LOVE UNDER DIFFICULTIES—BOB DALTON'S
HEART CLEAN GONE—THE WILES AND WAYS OF A
COUNTRY COQUETTE—COURTING BY THE ROAD-
SIDE—AN OUTSIDER THE FAVORITE—THE
MURDEROUS GLEAM IN THE RE-
PULSED LOVER'S EYE—A VIL-
LAGE ROMEO KILLED BY AN
INFURIATED RIVAL.

———

It has been often and truthfully said that love
acts the same within the bosom of a country girl
and that of a great lady. In both cases it runs its
own, obstinate course, no matter the obstacle, and
perfectly mindless of the sorrows and wraths it does
arouse on its way.

When Minnie Johnson, the only daughter of
Mother Dalton's deceased sister and brother-in-law,
had found a shelter under her aunt's roof, some five
years previous to the beginning of this narrative, it
would not have been a hard thing to guess that one

of her stalwart cousins would be sure to fall in love
with the maiden, when her bright country beauty
would have reached blooming time.

Nor would it have been overstraining the prob-
abilities to suppose that the said sweet maiden
would have returned the sentiment and become, at
the right moment, the blushing bride of her tall
sweetheart.

Such would have been the *natural* course of
things; needless to add that it was all to turn out
very differently.

That is, the part played by the girl was to be
strangely in variance with the outlined plot.

The part ascribed to the cousin-lover *did* follow
but too faithfully the beaten path, and Bob Dalton,
for the last six months, had been over head and ears
in love with that little heartless coquette of a country lass, the sprightly, saucy, thoughtless Minnie
Johnson.

On his duties in the territory, he had now been
absent for over six weeks, and during this lapse of
time an event of grave import had taken place.

A new suitor had appeared upon the field—or
rather within the farm limits of old Louis Dalton—
and like Cæsar he had come, seen and conquered.

Minnie Johnson was not heart-free any longer; the massive figure and engaging manners of Charley Montgomery had done their work and driven away whatever affectionate feeling her cousin Bob Dalton had inspired her with.

And it was the first time since that momentous change had taken place in the girl's life, that Bob and Minnie were again reunited in the old place by the Missouri Pacific R. R. tracks.

With the calm duplicity natural to her sex, the girl walked into the room, smiling and cordial as ever, allowing herself to be kissed all round by her four stalwart kinsmen. Bob had his share of the feast, but no more.

After a few moments of desultory questioning and jesting, the lover anxiously awaited an occasion to slip out of doors with his little sweetheart, whom his brothers had always considered as being to a great extent "Bob's girl." She had until then accepted the situation gladly enough and visibly encouraged her cousin's persistent attentions.

But on that day, without putting into it any affectation of coolness, Minnie managed to keep either in the sick room with Si, or in the kitchen with Mother Dalton, or among the men together.

Not a chance did she give Bob for the little tete-a-
tete that had made his mouth water, in advance,
when riding on the long way home. When evening
came on, after the family supper, she spoke of the
night before she had spent awake by the child's
bedside, and slipping out very soon after entered
her own little den and locked the door behind her,
with a general "Good-night, boys, and pleasant
dreams."

The disconsolate Bob could hardly hide his cruel
mortification. He now realized full well that something or somebody must have stepped between "his
girl" and himself and caused this painful estrange-
ment. Who it could be he failed to imagine, but
his jealousy was of course awakened and he set upon
right away questioning his mother.

"What's the matter with the girl?" he brusquely
asked, after he had been darkly brooding in his solitary corner for the best part of an hour.

There was a general silence in the living room, for
all the brothers were too closely bound together not
to take the deepest interest in whatever affected any
of them.

"Nothing much, I guess; she is that tired though
from watching over Si, day and night, when I am

doing the chores about the place. I guess that's all—"

"Then she hasn't been keeping company with any new fellow, since I was here last?" was the next abrupt question. The old woman fidgeted about, visibly troubled.

A voice that had hardly been heard the whole of that afternoon, that of the taciturn, sullen farmer, arose now from his favorite corner near the fire-place.

"What's the use of lying to the boy, mother? Let him have the truth right now and be done with it—"

"Just like you, dad," cried his querulous spouse, "to speak only to bring about trouble. What of it if the girl has been out a few times with that Charley Montgomery—"

"Hold on; is that the man's name?" was Bob's stern question.

"That's the name he goes by, so far as I know," the mother answered, rather sheepishly, "but I tell ye it's just a passing fancy of the girl; nothing to get worried about, Bob."

The boy bit his lips angrily and kept silent. Just then Grat queried:

"I used to know a man by the name of Mont-

gomery who made a living by peddling whisky all
through the Cherokee Nation. If he is the same
man he has had several months' acquaintance with
the Fort Smith jail. He is a tough and a sneak,
that's what he is—"

"Remember anything particular about his face?"
asked the *pater familias*, who seemed strangely
interested in the subject.

"Well, he had a rather promine t nose, with a
wart on the left side of it."

"That's our man," quoth Louis Dalton, curtly.
"He is working now for Ted Seymour."

"West of the Santa Fe tracks?"

"Yep."

At that moment, Bob rose with an ominous
gleam in his eyes.

"Guess, I'll take a walk," he said, picking his wide-
brimmed hat that lay on the floor by the side of his
Winchester.

Nobody spoke; but every one understood. The
boy's untamable temper was well known to all
present.

"I'll go along," said Emmet.

"All right; don't you fret mother, we'll be back
soon. We'll just take the lay of the land—"

And Bob laughed a loud, dreary laugh.

As the two boys stepped out in the yard, they noticed a light still burning in Minnie's room. The rough wooden shutters were closed but the gleam filtered through the cracks. That set Bob a-thinking.

He walked to the window and knocked at it rather gently, considering his excitement.

No answer came. He knocked louder and louder.

No answer yet. The truth came to him like a flash.

The girl was out. She had gone to meet her lover to warn him to keep away for a while—

Turning about with a smothered oath, Bob said to Emmet:

"Let us get on her trail—we have to find her— and pretty quick, too."

The younger boy nodded silently. His keen look, accustomed for years to the adventures of out-door life, had instantly noticed fresh footprints close to the window. He followed them up across the yard in the direction of the cornfield behind. A brilliant moonlight allowed the young men to keep the trail in clear sight for almost a quarter of a mile. Then a creek came across the track and they had to use their own judgment.

It was not much of a distance to Ted Seymour's place, a large, prosperous-looking group of buildings, on the South side of Coffeyville.   This mile or so was covered with incredible rapidity by the excited lover and his faithful chum.   When they reached the place, the living house, a two-story building of fair size and aspect, was wrapped up in darkness; evidently every one in it had retired for the night.

Repeated knocking and loud calling finally caused one of the upper windows to be opened, and an angry voice shrieked:

"What's this—of a tantrum about? We ain't keeping a hotel, to be waken up at all hours.   What you want?"

Bob answered promptly:

"We are two of the Dalton boys, and we have got a pressing message for Charley Montgomery. Excuse the trouble, boss, but we *must* see him at once.   It's news that won't keep waiting."

"It is, is it?" was the gruff answer.   "Then you better walk over to that big barn, over there to the right, and knock till the fellow wakes up.   That's where he sleeps."

"Thanks, Mr. Seymour; excuse the trouble. won't you?"

"I guess I'll have to, anyway. Good-night, boys;" and with a loud, not unpleasant laugh, the master of the place let down his window with a bang.

Two minutes later, the Daltons were executing a regular tattoo upon the big barn door. Inside it sounded as hollow as a bass-drum; but it seemed untenanted by any living being except corn-rats, which were seen scampering away like mad, disturbed in their nightly repast.

Suddenly Emmet discovered that the door was not closed. It had simply been pushed back, and a piece of wood slipped under it from the outside to keep it from turning on its hinges. Around it, recent footprints were clearly visible.

To open the door and rush into the building was but the matter of a few seconds.

Bob leading, the two brothers climbed the ladder at the further end of the barn and reached the hay loft, where they supposed the man they were after to be located.

Through the upper opening the light of the moon threw a white glare of such intensity that every corner of the place was as easily inspected as in full daylight.

And one glance was enough to tell the boy that the loft was empty of its occupant.

But on the floor, just close to the window, there lay a little heap of some red silken stuff.

Picking it up, Bob cried out with a fearful oath:

"G—— —— it! That's the kerchief I gave Lizzie at the last County Fair!"

The girl had been there, notified her lover of the dangers ahead, and now they had both doubtless fled to parts unknown, away from jealous cousins and possible bloodshed.

The bell of a locomotive dragging a heavily loaded train along the Santa Fe track broke the dread silence brought about by this cruel revelation. It was the night Express to Kansas City, just leaving Coffeyville.

And as the boys gazed with excited attention at the line of cars filing but a dozen yards away, fate would have it that Bob's eyes fell upon the form of his faithless sweetheart sitting close to the big burly Charley Montgomery, on her way to undisturbed bliss.

With a curse that almost froze the blood in Emmet's veins, accustomed though he was to the fearful oaths of his habitual associates, cow-boys and scouters, Bob rushed down the stairs like mad, and fired after the flying train every shot in his Winchester.

Then, without noticing the wild disturbance this insane feat of his was creating over Ted Seymour's whole establishment, the boy ran through the fields uttering half in articulate threats of direst vengeance.

Seven weeks later, on a dark December night, stormy and drear, Charley Montgomery, who had come back to his old boss just for a day to get his back pay and his few traps, having been told that Bob Dalton was away in the territory, was shot in the back near the very same barn and fell dead from a single wound.

How the murderers disposed of the corpse has been told in our first chapter. What influence this first crime and the ferocious motive that inspired it were to have upon the Dalton boys' lives will never be clearly elucidated.

Suffice it to know that the treachery of his first love threw Bob Dalton into that criminal existence which was to end in his tragic death, but a short mile from the scene of his first deed of blood.

CHAPTER IV.

THE LAW'S DEFENDERS—OPENING OF THE OKLAHOMA
TERRITORY, APRIL 22, 1889—LICENSE AND CRIME
RUNNING RIOT—HOW WRETCHEDLY UNCLE SAM
REWARDS HIS SWORN SERVANTS—U. S.
DEPUTY MARSHALS AND THEIR ILL-
PAID LIVES OF CONSTANT PERIL
—THE WATCH-DOGS TURN-
ING WOLVES.

On the 22d of April, 1889—a day ever to be
remembered by the present generation of settlers in
the glorious Southwest—the bugles, all along the
line of the excited crowd camping upon Kansas
ground, sounded the signal that opened the new
territory of Oklahoma to the incoming of settlers.

In addition to furnishing to the farmer a mag-
nificent soil, unsurpassed even by the Illinois bottoms
in productiveness, and so favorably situated that it
was then and there ready for the plow, being free of
rock, swamp or forest, this superb addition to the

public lands of Uncle Sam is blessed with a climate so exquisitely balanced between the long winters of the North and the long summers of the South, that almost all the products of both North and South can be successfully cultivated.

And the people far and wide knew of the natural wealth this new Canaan was to open to the happy owners of the coveted lands and, for weeks, had been camping all along the frontier, every son and daughter of them thrilling with excitement at the thought of claiming the benefit of the generous Homestead Law, and of staking valuable claims in the close neighborhood of the projected cities.

Since other such openings will be offered from time to time in the same vicinity to those willing to avail themselves of the privileges so freely granted by Uncle Sam, we may just as well state here the leading conditions that render such claims valid and transferable.

The lands entered in a claimant's name in the land offices of either Guthrie, Oklahoma City, or Kingfisher, must be resided upon and improved for not less than fourteen months, but the settler may delay making final proof for five years. The extraordinary low price to be paid for such fertile land is

$1.50 per acre, of which amount one-half only has to be paid cash down; the rest within two years. Land office fees for entering 160 acres, $14.00. Final proof fee, $4.00.

When one considers that at the present day, just three years and a half after the reservation was thrown open for settlement, a claim of 160 acres, within the limits of the city of Guthrie, which must have cost to the original owner a total sum (including all fees) of $258.00, part of which he did not even have to pay until April 1891, is worth now all the way from one hundred thousand to a quarter of a million dollars, it is easy to understand with what furious greed the sixty thousand would-be settlers, who rushed in like a living torrent on that memorable day, must have been urged almost to any deed of violence. To take and keep possession of desirable city lots or particularly well situated farm-land; to have one's entries made upon the official records—those two ambitions which might, if successfully attained, make a Crœsus out of a pauper, aroused within this motley and decidedly wild assemblage the worst passions dormant within every human being.

And how was the law prepared to resist and quell

the riotous propensities of this crowd, excited ten-fold by the rowdy element that is ever sure to be mixed, in a large proportion, with the peaceful citizens upon business bent?

It may just as well be stated, right here, that *it was not prepared at all.* In fact *law*, in the usual meaning of the word, did not *exist* within the new territory for a full twelve-month, that is, until Congress passed, in March, 1890, a bill establishing a United States Court, whose jurisdiction was to extend over the whole of the Indian Territory, Oklahoma included.

Until then, and during this whole year of unprecedented excitement, the only guardians of the public peace were a few men of incredible intrepidity, with U. S. Deputy Marshals' badges pinned to their coats, and whose indefatigable energy managed to keep within bounds the thousand and more desperadoes, thieves and outlaws that had chosen to make the new territory the stage upon which to pursue their criminal careers.

Of course the early settlements that were to become within a year populous and thriving cities, with churches, schools, hotels, brick business blocks and charming private residences, such cities as

Guthrie, the capital of the territory, Oklahoma City,
Kingfisher, etc., were then but large agglomerations
of tents or hastily-built shanties, amid which grog-
sellers, faro dealers, monte sharp swindlers and
lewd women of the worst description thrived and
grew fat out of their nefarious traffic.

Promiscuous shooting, either to kill or simply for
the amusement of drunken revelers, was heard day
and night.   Around the tracts of land specially coveted, regular free fights would take place with
bowie-knives, revolvers, and even Winchesters,
called into frequent and bloody use.

Think of the situation of the honest and respectable citizen who had collected his little whole, and,
gathering his wife and children about him, had
driven over the limits at a great expense of money
and greater expense of fatigue and privations!
Now, he was here, on the ground; his troubles ought
to have been at an end, and the blessed moment
when he would set his foot upon the land that was
to be his according to the terms of the law, had come
at last.   But ruffians had taken good care that his
pains should count him for nothing; what they could
not pilfer stealthily, they would rob with guns in
their hands; and driving him into the wilderness

again, impudently claim ownership over the very
claim he had staked himself. Where was help to
come from for the unfortunate? How was peace
with honor to be restored to him again? All praise
to those noble fellows who threw themselves forward with clear heads, stout hearts and robust mus-
cles to drive away the miscreants! There shall not
be said enough, by half, as an acknowledgment for
those services rendered by that handful of the law's
intrepid defenders. If Oklahoma counts now among
the most prosperous regions of this blessed country
of ours, let it be known far and wide that it is due to
the bravery of those few Deputy Marshals who strug-
gled and fought and won the battle of order over
anarchy waged under its most hated and reckless
form.

Among them the names of Ransom Payne, Geo.
D. Thornton, Ed. Short—those two killed in the
discharge of their sworn duty—Frank Kress, O. S.
Rarick, C. F. Concord, John Swayne and scores of
others who took part, from 1889 to 1892, in this constant warfare for the good cause, ought to be associated with that of U. S. Marshal Grimes and Chief
Deputy Madsen.

We shall have occasion to relate, in connection

RANSOM PAYNE.

The United States Deputy Marshal, who kept on the trail
of the Dalton Gang for over Two Years.

with the criminal deeds of the Dalton gang, many of
the feats to the credit of that small troop of noble
men.

But, before returning to our "mutton," as the
French say, we shall have to make the reader cog-
nizant of one incredible feature in relation with the
heroic work done by U. S. Deputy Marshals in
the half-settled regions of the Southwest. We refer
to the pecuniary compensation those men receive at
the hands of Uncle Sam, for their risking their lives
in the defense of peace and property.

The figures we insert here, and which can be
relied upon as being absolutely correct, are so
absurdly small that they are almost sure to bring an
exclamation of indignant incredulity out of the
reader's mouth. Here they are, though, and Truth
itself.

For arresting a suspected or guilty party the U.S.
Deputy Marshal receives the munificent sum of
two dollars! And remember that, out there, he faces
death with every arrest, and remains, besides, the
marked victim of the arrested outlaw's friends. But
let us proceed.

The Deputy Marshal is allowed *six cents per mile*
when on the trail after a criminal, all expenses of

transportation, board, etc., to be paid by him out of these six cents.

When he returns with his two-dollar prisoner in charge, he is allowed *ten cents*, and has to feed and transport himself, the assistants he may require, and the prisoner himself, all at his (the Deputy Marshal's) own expense.

Now listen; this is not all. When the accounts are rendered, the Marshal deducts thirty-five per cent. of the gross amount *as his fee*. Then the bill is sent to Washington and—sometimes allowed!

In the meantime, the Deputy Marshal has had to advance all the money spent, borrowing it from friends—or usurers; very happy he is indeed if he finally gets in hard cash *just one-half* of what is legitimately due him.

And, mind, the man receives *no salary!*

So that in reality, besides the danger to life and limb he runs, every day the sun rises above the horizon, this valiant protector of the law in the Indian and Oklahoma territories runs another ghastly danger: that of actually starving for want of necessary sustenance.

And now, can any one be much surprised to hear that once in a while one of these courageous men, so

shabbily treated by their own country, falls from grace and enters the ranks of the malefactors he has spent the best years of his life hunting down through the region in his charge? It is an exceptional occurrence, mind, a most exceptional one; but human nature is not adamantine; it will succumb when the tentation of evil-doing grows in the same proportion as the reward for well-doing decreases almost to nothingness. Then, it's mighty hard, isn't it? to be month after month deprived of all the comforts, even the necessaries of existence, while around you crowds of loafers, who cleverly evade the clutches of the law, live on milk and honey pilfered right and left. Of course there's no paliating the dishonor attached to the act of stepping out of the ranks of the law's guardians to turn out one of its professional violators. But as He said, in his tender, merciful way:

"Let he who has never sinned throw the first stone."

Bob Dalton had for over a year followed in the honest footsteps of his brother Frank, and seen him, under his own eyes, fall the victim of desperadoes he was bent upon capturing. He had liked the adventurous life of the bold Deputy Marshals,

always on the go, always on the alert, breathing
God's pure air of liberty on the limitless plains.
He had learned then how to exist with little food
and less sleep; how to counterplot the schemes of
the wily criminals; and there was no guilty secret, no
trick of those nefarious trades he had not been taught
to fathom.   Just then he was ready to graduate as a
full-fledged defender of the peace, or a most dangerous enemy of society.   The knowledge acquired
could serve him both ways, and had he found in the
career of an officer the wherewithal to satisfy, within
certain limits, the love of pleasure lads of his age
cannot escape, doubtless that he would have finally
settled down as a man to be trusted and to be even
proud of.

But the $2.00 for each captured prisoner, the *six*
cents traveling money, and the *ten* cents return sub-
sidy, seemed to grow smaller and smaller as his
appetite grew larger and larger.   Around him
abounded the occasions for illicit gains; as an officer he could hope for a while to escape discovery,
and he doubtless succeeded more than once in sup-
plying the Indians with the whisky the law forbids
selling to them.   This was his first downward step.
Already the deed of blood of the preceding fall, the

consequences of which he and his brother had almost miraculously escaped, had given him a foretaste of the fascination of outlawry.   He felt like the lion-whelp which has tasted human flesh for the first time; it thirsts after more warm blood, and generally gets it.

An incident we are about to relate, trifling in appearance, but decisive in its consequences, was the last drop that caused the glass to overflow.

CHAPTER V.

BOB DALTON RECRUITS HIS GANG—THE BRAWL IN THE
GAMBLER'S DEN IN KINGFISHER—SHOOTING TO
KILL—A BROTHER OFFICER LEFT BEHIND, A
CORPSE—BOB A BORN LEADER OF MEN—
HORSE STEALING AS A LIVING—"ON
THE SCOUT" FOR GOOD.

About that time, Ben Dalton, the eldest of the
ten brothers, who had always stuck to the legitimate business of farming, although with only
moderate success, settled down with his mother
upon a claim he had staked in the vicinity of the
new city of Kingfisher. He is living there yet and
attending faithfully to the duties of his calling.
Father Louis Dalton, who had always proved a
steadily unsuccessful man, and whose temper had
been soured to such a point that he had turned a
regular man-hater, did not linger long upon the new
plan but soon returned to Coffeyville, where he lived
for a while doing odd jobs about the country, finally
dying in the early part of 1890.

Ben, although disapproving the roaming disposition of his younger brothers, had of course no
authority to hinder them from shaping their lives
according to their own fancies.   He, kindly enough,
kept a home for them to visit at times and recuperate,
and the mother stuck steadfastly to her great love
for "her boys," whom she doubtless remembered as
wee little tots, in tattered garments, gambolling
about her in the old, happy days of her comparative
prosperity.

The Kingfisher farm was of course a very primitive building, but it was prettily located near a
green-encased creek, and was sheltered from view
by a number of full grown trees. The causeway
was over two miles away, and, taken altogether,
the place was retired and quiet enough. Perhaps
when Bob and Grat had selected the spot, at the
time of the general invasion, they had shrewdly surmised the possibility of the place becoming for
them, later, a safe temporary refuge, when hardly
pressed by pursuers.

Be it what it may, one morning, almost at dawn
of day, toward the end of summer, 1889, three riders
were seen approaching cautiously the vicinity of
the Dalton farm. Their horses seemed jaded and

nearly ready to break down, and steeds and riders were bespattered with mud; for it had been raining heavily for several hours and the waves of dust had been transformed into mire pools. The men wore wide-brimmed slouch hats and had big boots on their feet. Winchesters and heavy revolvers constituted their visible weapons, and they formed altogether a pretty formidable troop. One of them, a beardless fellow, looking hardly more than twenty, but who seemed by common consent to be the leader, stopped the horses short, saying in a quiet voice:

"Here is the place—now you stay there, boys, under cover, and I'll reconnoiter. If the family is alone, will stop in for an hour's rest. The poor beasts need it;" and he patted affectionately his horse's neck. The brute seemed to like it and half turned its head in recognition. Bob and his horse— for the young man was none other than Bob Dalton himself—were evidently fond of each other.

"All right," said Grat, the oldest of the trio, getting off his steed and leading it to the creek near by. Emmet, also on foot, followed him silently, holding Bob's bridle, for his favorite brother had already wended his way toward the house.

A slender smoke above the trees indicated where the habitation was located and was sufficient evidence that somebody about the place was already up and doing. In fact, Bob had hardly reached the outskirts of the small clearing that surrounded the frame building than he noticed his mother standing in front of the open door, milking a cow.

A low and peculiar whistle on the boy's part caused the old woman to raise her head and gaze intently in the direction the well-known voice came from. The familiar form of one of her best-beloved children loomed up but a few rods away. She lost no time calling to him to come forward, and well knowing the ever cautious ways of his mother—she was not for nothing the aunt of the Younger brothers —the young U. S. Deputy Marshal now approached fearlessly.

After a hearty kiss to the "old woman" and a few words of hurried explanation, Bob retraced his steps in quest of his brothers, and, a few moments later, the three of them were gathered within doors and enjoying the first hearty meal spread before them for many hours. The horses, of course, had received their first and best care.

The story of their stealthy visit was told in a very

few words. They had taken part, the night before,
in a bloody affray in which, for the first time, they
had taken sides with some of their new friends
among the territorial outlaws and against the officers
of the law, their former associates; the latter had
been driven back, leaving behind one of their number, shot dead through the heart. The constable
had attempted, on that night, raiding a well-known
lair of robbers and whisky peddlers, and had met
with utter routing

The worse of the case was that the Daltons had
been recognized in that most objectionable company and were now constrained to throw the mask
and to give up serving two masters: Uncle Sam, that
paid them so ill, and the outlaw gang who offered
them such alluring inducements.

Some of the toughest characters in the region
were taking part in last night's revelry, that term-
inated in actual murder, and the Daltons had been
plainly recognized and even called by name with
amazed indignation by several of the officers who
later had made good their escape. So that they
must now be counted among those after whom the
marshal and his posse would be starting, that very
morning, in hot and revengeful pursuit.

The die was indeed cast; the bridges cut down behind the trio; they were to bloom now into full-fledged desperadoes, and, all other means of living being thus rendered unavailable by their own fault, they would have to find their subsistence as open and daring violators of the law.

With tears streaming down her wrinkled cheeks, did the poor mother listen to that terrible revelation. Ben stood by, sternly gazing at those once so promising lads who had decided to become the shame and grief of the family.

What was the use reproving them? Their bed was made, they had to lie on it now, and the first consequence of this awful night's work was to render them vagabonds upon the face of this great republic.

And so, the meal hastily eaten, and the horses barely rested, fed and watered, the boys kissed their afflicted parent, shook the hand of the bewildered eldest brother, and off they went toward one of those many out-of-the-way camping grounds they had often noticed when riding about as officers of the law.

Shortly afterward, large and systematic stealing of horses from the herds became more frequent than ever, and the new gang of thieves gained rapidly a

reputation of audacity unequaled in these parts. The rapidity of their movements and their surprising faculty of raiding one place while being almost seen at quite a distance from it, became the object of general fear and bewilderment among the cattle men and unfeigned admiration among outlaws and their ilk.

That admiration rendered, of course, very easy the recruiting of the troop of depedators soon dubbed "the Dalton Band," and which had instinctively and unanimously recognized for its chief and leading spirit Bob Dalton, the beardless youth hardly of age then. His shrewd and inventive genius, backed by an unbreakable spirit of intrepid determination, was a quality of such capital value to all men of his kind that they granted him enthusiastically the absolute obedience he expected from all men in his band.

His clear blue eyes had the steel glance before which everything and every one seemed to bow unwittingly. His riding was fearless and indefatigable; his shooting so sure that his marksmanship was the boast of all his friends. He could live on less food and less sleep than any brigand or law officer in these parts, and finally he possessed that mysterious

mastery over his fellow-beings which has been the vaunted privilege of but a few famous men. Besides, his courage awakened the enthusiasm of his "boys" who would have followed him—and did follow him, many and many a time, to death's door.

Three of them even fell by his side, without a hesitation or a murmur, when came the dread hour of final retribution—

Among the spots chosen by the new gang, which had rapidly grown in number, power and daring, for disposing of the products of its thefts, Baxter Springs was the settlement most generally selected; and so cleverly did Bob organize his raids that the robbers generally managed to get rid of their ill-gotten spoils before the first rumor of the raid had gained much headway. Besides, there are always in the territories and the bordering states of Kansas, Texas, Arkansas, people of doubtful honesty ready to drive any specially good bargains without too close inquiry. All they want is to be safe against any legal complication; and, as they pay their queer customers but a very small fraction of what the goods are worth, the profits compensate them plentifully for the risk they run, as *de facto*, if not openly, receivers of stolen property.

After each particularly successful and productive raid, the boys would disperse for a while and spend a few days or weeks in some of the small border cities, where they could find all those low pleasures just made for them and their ilk. Most of them, of course, were wildly dissipated fellows, drunkards and gamblers to the core and addicted to every species of vice.

But to Bob Dalton's praise be it said, he seldom plunged into those reeking abysses of iniquity, and always took good care to keep his young brother Emmet away from them. The leader had understood, from the start, that no such enterprise as the one he was managing at the peril of his life, could last for any time, with the ghost of a chance of success, if the chief and inspirer should have his brain habitually muddled by fiery drink and riotous living. So he decided to remain within bounds and to keep his head clear and sound on all occasions. To that pledge he remained true to his dying day.

The band had passed without much trouble through the winter of 1889-90, and the few fellows dropped on the way either through capture or desertion, had been quickly replaced by just as stout and determined chaps. For the ground over there,

in the territory, was, especially in those days, fertile in all kinds of outlaws, from the city-thief and
burglar too well known by the police of the
larger towns, to the miners and the cowboys " on
the scout," that is, having abandoned their regular,
honest trade, to pick up their livings in a life of wild
and criminal adventure.

But the spring opened disastrously for the Dalton gang, for Grat, one of its most trustworthy
members, fell into the clutches of the law—not
while acting in consort with his pals, but when
caught prowling about the large range of Charles
McLelland, a prominent cattleman of the territory,
evidently with a view of preparing some gigantic raid.

The U. S. Marshal was so elated by the capture
of so valuable a prize that he ordered a strong posse
to take the man to Fort Smith, Ark. The force thus
employed was so numerous and so vigilant, that the
gang who dogged their footsteps, day and night, until
they reached the Fort, failed to find an opportunity
to rescue their chief's brother. An attempt of the
kind not followed by success could only gravely
compromise the prisoner, against whom, after all,
stood only charges of a general nature as being one
of the members of the gang.

The fact is, that after keeping Grat three months in jail at Fort Smith, no true bill was found against him; and in spite of his detestable reputation, the horse thief, not yet grown to his full stature as one of the most dangerous bandits of the age, was allowed to go scot-free, and was soon ready for more distinguished feats in the annals of crime.

Only, this time, Bob and he and Emmet thought prudent to make themselves scarce for a while, on the theatre of their recent outrages, and obeying some mysterious invitation—perhaps one from their brother William, settled at the time in California— disappeared suddenly this side of the Rocky mountains, and were heard and seen no more about their habitual haunts.

CHAPTER VI.

THE TULARE COUNTY RAID—AN EXPRESS TRAIN HELD
UP AT ALILA, ON THE MAIN LINE OF THE SOUTH-
ERN PACIFIC—POOR FIREMAN RADLIFF KILLED
BY MASKED ROBBERS—FIVE MEN IN IT; TWO
ARRESTED BY DETECTIVE WILL SMITH
AND HIS POSSE—THE REST ESCAPE—
NINE THOUSAND DOLLARS REWARD
OFFERED BY THE COMPANY—THE
CONVICTED GRAT DALTON LEAPS
FROM A RUNNING TRAIN

———

The Southern Pacific Express, which runs
through between San Francisco and New Orleans
and leaves the Golden Gate City at 9 A. M. daily, is
due at the small station of Alila, Tulare county,
about 9 P. M. In winter it is crowded with passengers for the famed resorts of Southern California,
and especially for the prosperous city of Los
Angeles, which it reaches at 7:45 the next morning.
The express car run by the Wells-Fargo Express

Company is generally freighted with valuables, money packages, etc. The line has the reputation of being secure from high-handed robberies, and there is really but a few spots where such attacks could take place with even a possibility of success, for of late years all this region has grown marvelously in wealth and population.

Tulare county, though, and especially the portion south of the city of Tulare, is mountainous and ill adapted to cultivation. Hence, its settlements are insignificant and rather far apart.

However, when the Atlantic Express left Tulare, on the night of February 6, 1891, no one on board felt the least apprehension on account of the few lonely canons the train would have to cross before reaching the plains of Kern county.

The porters in the sleeping cars had attended to their nightly duties, and all the passengers, with the exception of a few jovial fellows making merry in the smoking compartment, had retired within their berths, when the train which was to have passed the station of Alila without stopping slowed up gradually, and finally came to a standstill but a few rods from the little depot.

The conductor, an old hand ready for any emer-

gency, immediately stepped out to find out the motive of this unusual occurrence, but a dozen oaths of choice calibre and the random firing of a couple of Winchesters drove him back into the cars with a rush.

There was no mistaking the incident; it was a bona fide hold up; the train had been stopped for the purpose of robbery.

Stopping the train had been easy work. A red light had been procured from the frightened station agent; the wires, both ways, cut down to prevent any communication ahead or behind, and by waving the light in front of the incoming train, in accordance with the railway regulations, the engineer had reduced speed and finally stopped.

A second later, two men, wearing long black masks, had jumped on board the engine and covered both its occupants with their Colt revolvers.

Then, by a dodge rather new at the time and which seemed to have been the pet invention of Bob Dalton, another couple of robbers seized the fireman, ordered him to take down his coal pick, and placing him in front of the Express car door, had him notify the messenger within, that the door would be broken open at once if he did not open it

willingly. He was warned not to shoot as he might, and probably would, hurt the fireman and not the assailants.

No answer from the besieged man being vouch-safed the attacking party, the work of destruction began without delay, and the door, battered and broken, was soon a useless protection.

Then this gruesome thing happened—

Poor Geo. Radliff, the fireman, his task under dire threats accomplished, made a gesture the rob-bers doubtless interpreted as an attempt to join the messenger and defend the burglarized car. Instan-taneously a shot through the head threw the unfort-unate fireman on the ground, while a second shot killed him on the spot.

Then the work of pillaging began. The mes-senger, however, had managed to jump out on the other side and to take to flight in the underbrush. With him went the combination that would have opened the safe, and the iron chest was too solidly fixed to the floor to be moved one inch. Crowbars broke in the attempt to force it open and the rob-bers had not supplied themselves with dynamite.

So that after all the attacking party had to con-tent themselves with a few parcels, comparatively

valueless, and not caring probably to visit the inmates of the cars now thoroughly aroused and doubtless prepared for systematic resistance, they called away the engineer's guard, and firing in the air a few disappointed volleys ran away in the darkness, leaving behind them the corpse of poor Geo. Radliff, murdered in cold blood and without even the shadow of an excuse.

The victim of the bloodthirsty wretches was tenderly picked up by the engineer and by the messenger who had been hiding but a short distance away, and the train started again, in mourning for the honest fellow wantonly butchered.

The next few hours carried the news of this gory outrage all over the country, and the Southern Pacific R. R. Co.'s chief detective, William Smith, was, before morning, on the theater of the daring attack, with two carloads of horses and officers.

Aggregate rewards to the amount of nine thousand dollars were offered by both the railroad and the express companies. A hot pursuit began within eight hours of the perpetration of the crime, and by an unheard-of streak of luck two of the probably guilty parties fell into the hands of the police before the week was ended.

They proved to be a Californian gentleman of political prominence in those parts, by name William Dalton, and his brother, just fresh from the Indian Territory, and whose recent exploits were soon exposed—Grat Dalton himself.

Grat's horse had met with a severe fall shortly after the attack, and his master had been much bruised in the accident. Thinking himself absolutely unsuspected, since this was the very first raid attempted by his gang that side of the Rockies, he had boldly taken refuge upon his brother's place, in the same county of Tulare. A chain of circumstantial evidence traced him from the Alila canon to his present shelter, and the messenger and engineer both declared under oath that they had heard his voice on that eventful night of the 6th of February, and that his size and general outlines corresponded exactly with that of the robber left in charge of the engine.

This fact, of course, saved Grat from the gallows. as the shots that had killed poor Radliff had been fired by the men that stood about the express car.

On the other side, Will Dalton's political pull helped him, undoubtedly, to establish the alibi which made him an apparently total stranger to the

Alila hold-up. The fact of his sheltering his wounded brother, even coming to him under suspicious circumstances, could hardly be counted against him.

So that finally the Tulare county jury acquitted William Dalton, but found Grat Dalton guilty of complicity in the Southern Pacific R. R. robbery at Alila.

The judge sentenced Grat Dalton to twenty years in the state penitentiary.

And the convicted robber was about reaching his destination when another extraordinary occurrence changed once more the course of events, and set Grat one step nearer to the terrible death he was to meet twenty months later at the hands of the infuriated Coffeyville citizens.

Two deputy sheriffs had been entrusted with the task of bringing over Grat Dalton from the Tulare county jail to the state penitentiary. Knowing the man to be an athlete and a fearless desperado, they had decided to have his feet tied together with a leather thong, allowing their prisoner to take short steps only, while by turns each of the deputy sheriffs would link one of his wrists to one of the man s wrists by means of a double manacle. Thus

it seemed that no possible escape could be effected. By using a day-train full of people there was no danger of an attempt at rescue by Grat's confederates.

So the trio started on its trip on a fine morning in early April, 1891. The temperature was very hot, as it usually is at that time of the year all over southern California, and the window next to which sat the prisoner had been thrown open. While the train was running at full speed—forty-five miles an hour— between Fresno and Berenda, the deputy sheriff who was tied up to the prisoner felt so drowsy that he let his head droop upon his breast, while he sunk in a delightful doze. His companion was having a chat and a smoke with a friend at the further end of the car.

Suddenly Grat Dalton rose from his seat with a jerk that awoke his bewildered neighbor. By a magic that has never been explained to this day, the bracelet around the prisoner's wrist fell upon the seat, while the man himself pitched headforemost and with lightning rapidity through the open window. A great noise of water was heard outside, and the excited passengers, now all shouting and crowding to that side of the train, could just see the form

of the escaped prisoner swallowed up by the blue
waters of a running stream.

The whole thing had not lasted five seconds,
and the officers were gazing at each other with
comic desolation, without even thinking of having
the train stopped, when it slacked speed upon the
conductor's spontaneously pulling the bell-rope.

The deputy sheriffs started out in hot pursuit,
but their search was fruitless.

All they found on the river bank, close to the
point where this incredible plunge had taken place,
was the leathern thong and the fresh hoofprints of
a couple of horses that had evidently been kept
waiting for the prearranged escape of Grat Dalton.

PART THE SECOND.

CRIMINAL MEN.

CHAPTER I.

THE GANG'S LAIR—IN THE INDIAN TERRITORY AGAIN—
RANSOM PAYNE ON THE TRAIL—A HOT CHASE—
TIGER JACK'S DISCOVERY—THE OUTLAWS'
CAMP FIRE FOUND SMOKING YET—A NAR-
ROW ESCAPE FROM A SURE AND TER-
RIBLE DEATH—FOILED AGAIN.

The trial of Grat Dalton and the precise circumstantial evidence which had connected him with
the Alila, Tulare county, hold-up on the S. P. R. R. revived at once in the minds of the police force in the
Indian and Oklahoma territories the remembrance
of the various depredations traced to the Dalton
brothers during their last month's stay in the Southwest.

Although Grat had kept stolidly mum as to his
accomplices' names, decided as he was to face the

highest penalty of the law rather than peach upon his pals, the detectives in charge of the case reached rapidly the following conclusions:

Grat's brothers were with him in the Tulare county outrage;

And if the trio, now reconstituted through Grat's successful escape, were ever to be found and arrested, they must be looked for through the Indian Territory they knew so well, and where hundreds of friends, among the outlaws and the Redskins, would be only too proud to supply them with shelter and assistance.

Will Smith, the official entrusted by the Railroad Company and by Wells-Fargo's Express Company with the task of bringing the raiders to retribution, communicated at once with the Marshal of the Oklahoma Territory, and, as a consequence, the skilled, indefatigable and intrepid Deputy Marshal Ransom Payne was put in charge of the case, and directed to scour the country to get the three Daltons dead, or alive, into the clutches of the law.

Ransom Payne was already well known about the land as a fearless enemy of evil-doers and a shrewd discoverer of apparently lost trails.

He was a tall, strongly-built man of about forty.

with a fine, clean-cut face and a blonde moustache of
no mean proportions. He was born in 1850, in
Kappolo county, Iowa, but had been raised in the
state of Kentucky, where he had received an excellent common-school education. At the time of the
Tulare county outrage he had already resided in the
Southwest for about eight years, having been quite
successful as a real estate agent in the city of
Wichita, Kansas.

Since 1888, however, the attractions a life of exciting activity always exerts over the minds of brave
men, had induced him to enter the ranks of the
territorial force as U. S. Deputy Marshal, and as
such he had acted during the extraordinary period
that immediately followed the opening of the Oklahoma reservation—April 22, 1889.

The presence in the region of thousands of outlaws of every stamp and description, mingled with
the toughest kind of rumsellers, gamblers and fast
women, rendered almost superhumanly difficult the
task of the sixty men entrusted by Uncle Sam with
the charge of keeping a semblance of order amid
the sixty thousand new citizens of this extempor-
ized community; especially so on account of the
staking-out of claims bringing about constant and

bloody affrays between citizens otherwise respectable.

Two cases followed up to a successful issue by Ransom Payne and his chosen assistants attracted much attention at the time and deserve more than a passing notice in these pages, as they are typical of the state of semi-anarchy that reigned over the whole territory until Congress, in March, 1890, promulgated laws for the protection of property and its owners,

A veteran soldier, by name Captain Couch, was murdered by one J. C. Adams, the crime being the direct upshot of a disputed claim extending over part of the present city of Guthrie, capital of the territory, this piece of land being now valued over $250,000.

The murderer was tracked by Ransom Payne, arrested and brought to trial. The case cost the United States the snug sum of fifteen thousand dollars. Adams was convicted and sent to the Columbus, O., the nearest United States penitentiary, for a long term of years.

The details of this eventful pursuit and the recital of the deeds of extraordinary bravery to be placed to the credit of Ransom Payne and his posse would suffice to fill a volume.

Another case of mysterious and enthralling interest is that of the murder of Charley Grant by one Eddie Belden, on a farm near Edmund, Oklahoma Territory. Grant owned a valuable claim close by, which his chum and bosom friend, Eddie Belden, insisted he should sell to him. The young man persistently refused, and one night the two had a quarrel about it, and Grant was shot dead. His corpse was hidden under a pile of manure, and his disappearance was plausibly explained by Belden, who produced a document pretending to be signed by Grant and transferring to him, Belden, the fee-simple to the above-mentioned claim. The crime had been committed on the farm of a man named Holley, a brother-in-law of Belden. It was not long before Payne had ferreted out the guilty party, acting upon the well-known principle: "Look out for whomsoever is benefited by the crime."

Both Belden and Holley were arrested, not without the former showing fight. The body was discovered, recognizable yet, although in a fearful state of putrefaction, under the growing heap of manure; but the brother-in-law's complicity could not be established, as he protested his absolute ignorance in the matter. Eddie Belden, however, was convicted

of murder in the first degree, and sentenced to be hanged. The President of the United States commuted the dread penalty to imprisonment for life.

Ransom Payne, who had, pistol in hand, arrested the accused murderer, himself brought the sentenced man to Columbus, Ohio.

These are but two of the many dramatic incidents in the busy life of U. S. Deputy Marshal Payne; they are quoted only as displaying on his part, besides an unusual amount of intrepidity, a cool and discerning spirit that made him a sure and shrewd leader among the defenders of the law.

It explains how the marshal of the territory chose him, out of a number of reliable and courageous men, to trace the Dalton gang and bring it to book for its first railroad outrage and the wanton murder of poor George Radliff, the fireman of the S. P. R. R. Express.

After conferring with Will Smith, the California detective, who had come all the way to Guthrie to start the searching party on its work, Ransom Payne recruited with the utmost care a posse he could depend upon, and having laid in a sufficient supply of horses, guns, ammunition and provisions he started on the trail.

In the party thus formed were found such c, ol-
headed and determined men as Dodge, of the Wₜlls,
Fargo & Co.'s squad of officers; Hec. Thomas, an
experienced posse man; Burl Cocks, a tried U. S.
Deputy Marshal, and a faithful and intelligent full-
blooded Indian, Tiger Jack by name.

One day those five men, who had been for seventy-
two hours in hot pursuit of Bob Dalton, Emmet Dalton, and their most daring associate, Charlie Bryant,
stopped for dinner at the entrance of a canon in the
vicinity of the Cimarron river, also known as the
Red Fork of the Arkansas river.

It was early in May, 1889, the weather was beau-
tifully clear; there were plenty of trees about, afford-
ing a cooling shade, and the men, cracking jokes
and exchanging anecdotes about their various experiences, went on preparing their meal according to
the customary camp method. They hurried through,
as they knew the trail to be fresh and their objective
enemies but a few miles distant at most.

When they were about saddling their horses
again and starting on their man-hunt again, they
noticed Tiger Jack, the Indian follower they had
taken along with them, wildly running from the
mouth of the canon, his arms playing the windmill

act in a half insane fashion. He kept mute, though, until he had come up with them, and they cautiously imitated his silence.

His tale was a startling one and showed how narrowly the party had escaped wholesale slaughter. Without trying to imitate Tiger Jack's queer lingo, we'll just give his story as follows:

"I thought," said the man, "that while you were finishing dinner, I would go around a little and see how clear the trail was through the canon. I walked on, in the underbrush, very slow and quiet like, until suddenly I thought I smelt horses to windward. You know I can smell them a couple of miles ahead when the wind blows the right way. True enough, as I crept a few yards farther, now flat on my belly, I discovered three men grouped behind a stone ledge, to the right of the path we should have been sure to follow. We couldn't have seen them, you know, until passing a few feet from their hiding place."

"Then our fate was settled, boys," said Ransom Payne; "we should have been shot down like rabbits, every son of a gun of us— I guess Jack saved our lives, that's what he did."

The men were too startled yet to properly manifest their gratitude. Burl Cocks asked:

"And while you were watching them, did you notice that they were aware of our presence?"

"No doubt about that, captain; they must be kept posted along by some of those d— friends of theirs. But I think they were preparing to go, for the horse I saw was ready saddled and there was some cautious moving behind the ledge—"

"The best way to find out, without letting them have the fun of shooting us down from their vantage ground," suggested Dodge, "would be to climb the hill just above their camping place, instead of kindly passing under fire of their cursed Winchesters."

"Right you are, Sam," said Payne; "let us follow your plan; Tiger Jack and I shall precede the party about one hundred and fifty feet. We'll soon find out."

The party did not linger any longer around their smoldering fire, and proceeded on their march, in the order indicated. Some hard climbing amid the brush and loose stones brought them under cover directly above the spot where Tiger Jack had discovered the robbers' ambuscade.

But as their eyes plunged down upon the clever hiding place, they discovered at once that it was deserted—

The birds had flown; doubtless finding retreat the better part of valor, the possibility of the posse coming down upon them from above not escaping their practical judgment.

And when Ransom Payne and his men, after searching the woods with systematic caution, had come together again, just behind the ledge where their mortal foes had stood in wait for them, they found there, besides the remnant of a hearty meal and the hoofprints of several horses, two packages of cartridges, an overcoat and, stranger still, a live but maimed horse, with his saddle and trappings all complete—

Once more the courageous representatives of the law had been foiled by their dangerous adversaries —poor Geo. Radliff's death remained yet to be avenged.

CHAPTER II.

The village of Kingfisher, one of the creations of
the recent settlement in the Oklahoma reservation,
has grown already to the dignity of a full-fledged city.
A United States Land Office is located there, and a
great deal of visitors having business with it are found
in its neatly kept hotels. Stores and amusements
such as are appreciated among this class of people,
are found here in plenty, and the tone of the popu-

lation is rapidly growing better and steadier. The rowdy element has had to give up the struggle and make itself scarce, although of course, it is represented there yet by tough characters and a strong heavy drinking and gambling element.

Among the business men themselves, a few may be found who tolerate, if they don't openly sympathize with, whatever there is left of rampant lawlessness. Half out of fear, half on account of the pecuniary benefit they derive from having those men as regular customers and often enough sharing their illegal profits, they will at times be caught in rather doubtful transactions which place them under the law's hand. It is especially so when they happen to be related by family ties with some of the desperadoes who still infest this otherwise highly prospelous section of the country.

As was stated in one of our preceding chapters, Mother Dalton's only surviving daughter had been married for some time to a well-to-do butcher of Kingfisher, a man called Whipple. When the attention of the officers began to be directed toward the Dalton boys' criminal operations, and especially after the Tulare county hold-up, and the murder of George Radliff and the daring escape from custody

of Grat Dalton, a very strict, although secret, watch
had been established, not only around Ben Daltons'
farm, upon which, as we know, resided, and resides
to this day, the boys' mother, but also upon the
movements and surroundings of Whipple, the
butcher, married to a Dalton girl.

Nothing, however, of a particularly suspicious
nature warranted, for awhile, the police's interference in the brother-in-law's affairs, until, one day,
this worthy returned from a business trip riding a
horse nobody in town knew him to possess. He
declared that he had bought this horse during his
trip, and nothing more would have been thought of
it, if, shortly afterward, Fred Carter, a cattle man of
Beaver county, happening to pass in front of Whipple's store, had not recognized in the horse tied to a
hitching post and awaiting his new master, a horse
stolen from him, with several others, a couple of
months earlier by Bob Dalton's gang. He had even
been told that Bob was particularly fond of the
beast, and had sung its praises over and over again.

Having called at the U. S. Deputy Marshal's
office, to have a talk with him concerning the
matter before asking a justice of the peace for a
writ of replevin, Fred Carter met there Ransom

Payne, on a searching tour, down from Guthrie, his home. The men compared notes, and the officers, clearly remembering the version of the purchase as given by Whipple to his friends and the public, concluded that there was here something that needed immediate explanation and might lead to a series of startling and most useful discoveries.

A cautious inquiry was set on foot, Fred Carter being recommended in the meantime to keep his own counsel and not allow any one to know of the proposed proceedings.

The information collected proved sufficient to establish a *prima facie* case against Whipple, of receiving and keeping stolen goods knowing the same to be stolen; and later on, the same night, the two U. S. Deputy Marshals, who had sworn the necessary warrants, pounced upon Whipple as he was returning to his home, a short distance from the city, riding the very steed Fred Carter claimed as his own. That same night, the prisoner, the complainant, the two officers and the horse, were carried over the Rock Island R. R. to Wichita, Kas., the nearest United States jail, where Whipple was soon securely locked up.

The arrest had been made with such secrecy and

with such lightning rapidity, that the population of Kingfisher was absolutely dumbfounded when they heard of it.

Mrs. Whipple, *nee* Dalton, was alone in the store, weeping violently and protesting her husband's absolute innocence. She received the condoling visits of her neighbors and friends, and soon decided to proceed with business with the help of her assistants, proposing later in the day to start for Wichita, bringing to her husband the necessary money to fight the case to the bitter end.

Doubtless the Dalton brothers must have been just at that time in hiding but a short distance from their mother's farm, or the telegraphic news of their brother-in-law's arrest must have reached them almost as once, for a written, although unsigned message, clearly emanating from the redoutable trio reached, within twenty-four hours, the Kingfisher civic authorities.

It read as follows:

"You are making d—— fools of yourselves if you think you can tackle any of our people without putting yourselves in a —— of a fix. That Ransom Payne 'll have to swing for it, sure, or to have so much lead pumped into his d—— carcass that his

own mother won't know him.   Let those that are called as witnesses beware!"

And underneath, they had rudely drawn a skull and cross bones with these words in big red letters:

"WE SHOOT TO KILL!"

The mayor and police captain of the village found it useless to rouse the frightened anxiety of the population by allowing this scurrilous epistle to be generally known. They simply increased the precautions generally taken by them to prevent any outrage against the lives and property of the citizens to be perpetrated, and kept a close watch upon gambling dens, groggeries and houses of evil-resort where the Daltons counted numberless friends but too ready to help them in any pillaging or burning of houses.

The Kingfisher officials were soon relieved, however, of this new load of anxiety by the news that Whipple had been let go scot free, his wife's active interference having caused the withdrawal of the complaint.

But the very same day this announcement was made to the public, thus removing the probability of a revengeful and murderous attack upon the city on the part of the Dalton gang, the telegraph wires

flashed the astounding news that the desperadoes had resumed their railroad holding-up operations, and, true to their oath of getting even with Ransom Payne, had combined "business with pleasure" and stopped the very train upon which the faithful officer was returning from his Wichita trip, en route to his Guthrie home.

And in the saloons of Kingfisher that night, the ruffian element, enthused by the proud record their favorites were making, were crying out boastfully, speaking in the absent desperadoes' name:

"Don't you see, they are 'fraid of us!"

CHAPTER III.

In the councils of the band, Bob more in control than ever, it had been resolved to strike a great and resounding blow, in the midst of the region that knew them so well but had never seen them yet at work upon any really startling affair.

A hold-up of the first class taking place upon the territory itself would place their gang right away in the front rank among those associations of malefactors, the very name of which inspires terror

BRODWELL   BOB   GRAT   POWERS

JOHN J. KLOEHR
The heroic liveryman who shot dead
Bob Dalton, Grat Dalton and Bill Powers

and secures for their members a success based on
other people's cowardice.   In other words, they
would be able, henceforth, to stop trains, raid banks
and march, in broad daylight, through closely-inhab-
ited settlements, without any one even daring to raise
a finger or pull a gun.

Just then occurred the Whipple arrest, and Bob
declared that now was their opportunity to spread a
wholesome terror in the camp of the enemy.

First, they would boldly proclaim their intention
of getting even with those who had dared molest
the friendly butcher, their relative by marriage.

Then, they would manage to hit two birds with
one stone in holding up the very train containing
their arch-enemy, Ransom Payne, taking both profit
and revenge at one fell swoop.

This tremendously risky move was agreed upon
enthusiastically and an approximate date fixed
some time after the ending of the expected trial of
Whipple at Wichita.   That left the band several
days, weeks perhaps, for other minor business, and
they dispersed on their various criminal errands
bent.

Only Bob, Emmet, and Charlie Bryant remained
together on the watch, full arrangements having

been made to notify the rest of the band, in due time.

But things having turned entirely differently from what the gang expected, that is, Whipple having been released almost at once, Bob was notified, just a few hours ahead, of Ransom Payne's departure from Wichita, and of his being on board train No. 403, the Fast Texas Express of the Santa Fe R. R., en route to Guthrie. The Deputy Marshal was to leave at 5:45 P. M. that very night, and if he was really to be captured on his way home, the operations must be conducted with almost lightning rapidity.

The bold desperado was up to the emergency though, and he decided, on the spot, to "face the music," that is, hold up the train, rifle the express messenger's safe and secure possession, or shoot down in his tracks their indefatigable and unconquerable enemy, Ransom Payne. He would do it all with the two associates that were with him at the time—his brother Emmet and their trusted partner, Charlie Bryant.

An hour after the above information reached them, the three robbers had saddled their horses and were fleeing at their top speed toward the sta-

tion on the Santa Fe road, chosen by Bob as an appropriate point for a successful night attack.

It was the small Wharton depot in the Cherokee strip—about twenty miles from where the three men had been camping on the banks of the Red Rock creek, one of their favorite hiding places— that was selected by Bob; and toward it the men rode in post haste.

The time tables of the Santa Fe R. R., indicated that the Texas Fast Express would pass Wharton station at 10:13 P. M., but only stop there if properly signaled. For Wharton is not a center of population by any means, the whole agglomeration consisting of a small frame station and one or two general stores, with postoffice attachment.

However, the Wells-Fargo Express Company is represented there in the person of the station agent, and the Indian farmers and cattle men around patronize the station occasionally.

That night everything was more than usually quiet around the depot, when, toward 9:30 P. M., three horsemen rode to the door, and tied their horses to the hitching post.

It was Bob Dalton, Emmet Dalton and Charlie Bryant. Bob entered the station alone, the lower

part of his face muffled up, and his broad brimmed slouch hat brought down over his forehead. He stepped up to the solitary agent, and putting up his Winchester, said in a low but distinct voice:

"Get out on the platform and put up the signal for that train to stop."

The man opened his mouth and eyes wide in frightened stupefaction, then, closely followed by the desperado, walked out and fixed the signals as told.

He was then marched back in short order within the station, bound and gagged solidly in his little office and left to his own, not overpleasant, meditations.

In the meantime the two other robbers had patrolled the neighborhood and found everybody sound asleep and the couple of houses closed tight. No risk of any interference on the part of the baker's dozen of inhabitants, if they indeed counted up as high as that.

Then the trio prepared operations in earnest. The horses were led about a quarter of a mile back and tied there, while black masks came out of the men's pockets and were carefully placed over their features. Guns and revolvers being carefully in-

THE WHARTON TRAIN ROBBERY.—PAGE 97.

3

spected and found in prime order, the gang was now ready for the coming event.

All this had needed but a few minutes' time, and when the fast Texas Mail slowed up speed in obedience to the regular signals, its assailants stood ready to receive it.

But now we will let Ransom Payne himself, a passenger, as we said above, on board this unfortunate train, tell the story of the hold-up and the concomitant robbery.

"I had been slumbering for some time in the last car, in the rear, utterly fagged out by the preceding week's exertions, and truly delighted at the thought of reaching in a few more hours my cheerful home and my comfortable bed, when a sudden jerk told me that the train was stopping at some way station. There had been no hold-up in this neighborhood for a long while and my first thought was not one of alarm. However, I recollected at once that this night express, which I very frequently patronized, was but very seldom signaled to stop between Arkansas City and Guthrie. This stoppage awoke therefore my apprehensions and I tried to look out of the window to discover what the matter was. Suddenly a couple of shots sounded in the stillness of the night.

"It was all clear as a bell now. The Dalton boys had learned somehow that I was on the train and, true to their boast, they were coming on to "pump lead" into my unworthy—but decidedly precious—frame.

"Not a minute was to be lost. The fact of my having chosen the last car probably saved my life; for I could reach unnoticed the end of the car, which was at the same time the end of the train; and pulling out my trusty Colt, I slipped on the ground and walked noiselessly and under protection of the train, which lay between me and the robbers, toward the underbrush close to the track.

"There I stopped and stood in calm expectancy, resolved to sell my life dear if I should come to be discovered by the bandits.

"From the distance I could now hear the yells and the dreadful oaths of the scoundrels as two of them went through the cars, at breakneck speed, searching for me. I was told later that, according to the system they had practiced in Tulare county, they had taken the fireman down from the engine and had him act the coerced burglar.

"They soon gave up finding me, especially when conductor McTaggart swore, with a great deal of

well-assumed sang-froid, that I had missed the
train and was not to leave Kansas before morning.

"The brigands then concentrated their efforts
towards rifling the Express car. I was told since
that they only got $1,600 out of the safe and over-
looked a sack containing over $5,000 in silver.

"This time there was no bloodshed, and the whole
performance did not occupy thirty minutes. I
could see no trace of horses in the vicinity, although
the moon was so clear that one could have almost
read a newspaper by the light of its rays.

"The passengers, perhaps thirty or fifty in
number, half of whom were located in the sleeping
car, had been awakened of course by the noise of
the shooting; but obeying the conductor's advice,
which they doubtless did with great alacrity, they
remained quiet and hardly spoke above a whisper
until the train had been released by the gang.

"It was hardly eleven by my watch, when the
train steamed on, leaving me behind and alone in
this deserted spot. The situation was not so critical though, after all, for the desperadoes, who had
no idea of my being so near them, were not long
joining their horses—by the way, they passed just a
few feet from me—and I soon heard the hoofs

rapidly striking the dry ground. They were away and I was free to act.

"It did not take me two minutes to realize what to do next. I ran to the station, released the poor agent from his bonds and gag, and having repaired the north wire as best we could, I set him telegraphing to Wichita a short but pithy narrative of the hold-up. I asked for men and horses to begin a hot pursuit, and proceeded at once toward Orlando, the next station and a village of some two hundred people to gather among the brave fellows there the first elements of a posse.

"The next morning, at daybreak, a carload of men and horses reached Orlando from Guthrie; and having selected a set of men whose courage and indefatigable activity I could fully trust, I started before noon, on that day, on a furious chase that lasted over six weeks, and among the leading incidents, of which undoubtedly the most extraordinary was the death of Charlie Bryant, killed by poor Ed. Short, the best and truest of friends, in the discharge of his sworn duty."

CHAPTER IV.

———

The sensation caused all through the Indian and
Oklahoma territories and the neighboring states
of Kansas, Missouri and Texas, by the hold-up of
the Santa Fe Express at Wharton, Cherokee strip,
on the night of May 9, 1891, is yet in every one's
memory. It revived in the older folks the remembrance of the James Brothers' and Younger Brothers'
deeds of blood, and coupled with the Tulare county
outrage it gave rise to the gravest apprehensions.

It was useless to deny it any longer; a new gang.

under a leader of unusual daring and executive
ability, had come to the front, and would be sure to
attempt any crime to equal, if not surpass, the terrible fame left behind them by their predecessors.
The Daltons grew, almost in a week, to the proportions of full-fledged bandits of the most dangerous
stamp, and United States Marshal Grimes, in charge
of the Oklahoma Territory, realized that he must
send his best force on the trail and crush this new
power for evil that threatened to assume such re-
doubtable importance.

In such, not yet fully established communities, the
vigilant officers of the law are well aware of the
evil influence a few successful, unpunished crimes
of this particular stamp exert upon the imagination
of the younger, somewhat wild, element, not con-
taminated yet but too prone to be carried off by the
recital of deeds of extraordinary recklessness. The
tendency to instinctive imitation is rampant in the
human nature; especially so with young people accustomed to the open-air life and the rough existence of the cowboys and farmhands in the Southwest. If a gang of depredators be allowed to grow
in reputation, and manages, for a prolonged period,
to escape the clutches of the law, it either increases

and develops in enormous proportions, or it causes other similar gangs to be organized about the land with the avowed boast of throwing all past exploits into the shade.

And another very serious evil arises from the continuous existence of such bands of malefactors. As their deeds of blood are narrated about and of course magnified, from village to village and from insolated farm to lonely cattle range, the peacefully inclined citizens cannot help being filled with an increasing dread. The possibility of a raid haunts their sleep; and if by chance, the scoundrelly gang happens to call upon them for ammunition or victuals, they not only get the goods without paying for them but are often sheltered for a time against the pursuing posses. The excuse for such cowardly conduct evidently is, that the officers once gone and the small settlements left to themselves again, any refusal of help or any indication as to the whereabouts of the robbers is sure to bring down the bloody and prompt vengeance of the gang.

So, it comes to pass that the prolonged prosperity and impunity of any band of train robbers increases the amount of lawlessness rampant about,

and renders the citizens less and less of a help to the police force.

U. S. Marshal Grimes, alive to the gravity of the situation, telegraphed to his trusty lieutenant and deputy, Ransom Payne, pressing orders not to spare any effort to overtake the assailants of the Texas Fast Express and to gather in those other well-known members of the gang who did not happen to be present at the time of the Wharton outrage.

Such capital officers as George E. Thornton, E. D. Short, Frank Kress, Joe P. Jennings, George Orin Severns, were sent along to assist Payne, and, during those forty days of hard riding in pursuit of the desperadoes, other men were added to the posse, or took the places of the worn out ones.

But Ransom Payne went along, apparently impervious to exhaustion and collecting, on the way, with shrewd judgment, a mass of valuable information concerning the Daltons' habits and habitual rendezvous.

Love was again to play a part in this exciting frontier story, Bob Dalton a second time the hero of an amorous intrigue, but the triumphant hero, this time; no longer the rejected swain of a fickle little country lass.

"His girl," in this occurrence, was the tall, shapely, diamond-eyed sister of his chum and accomplice, Charlie Bryant.

She was a full blown beauty, and was said to be a grass widow from one of the Northern States. An expert on horseback; she handled a Winchester or a Colt with unfailing accuracy. Attracted by Bob's dash and imperious manner, she had thrown herself in his arms, so to speak, and, since his return from California, shared frequently with him the perils of his criminal enterprises.

But she soon found out that she could be of much more use to her lover and his companions, by keeping for them, always ready and well supplied with reserve horses, ammunition and provisions, a retreat which could be shifted from one corner of the county to another when the territorial police would get an inkling of its whereabouts.

Recently, that is a couple of weeks after the Wharton hold-up, Daisy Bryant, under the name of Mrs. Harry Jones, and with the demure ways of a Dakota widow in quest of a milder climate, had invested quite a snug little sum buying out an abandoned claim, a few miles west of Hennessey, in the Oklahoma Territory. She had found there a house

of some size, and the approaches of the place were such as to allow of an easy and far-reaching watch over all approaching visitors.

There had Bob, Emmet and Charlie Bryant found their devious way, and, remaining well under cover, managed to keep a riotous sort of a "good time." This lasted for three weeks at a stretch, and the funds were getting low again, and something had to be done soon to replenish the depleted exchequer. So Bob and Emmet started on a still hunt to pass the word to their principal associates, leaving behind, under his sister's roof, Charlie Bryant, who had not recovered yet from a first-class fit of delirium tremens, the consequence of long habits of inordinate intemperance.

We may just as well repeat right here, although we have mentioned the fact once before, that Bob Dalton had never been a heavy drinker, and had never allowed his younger brother to become one. That kind of prudence he had, to always keep his wits about him, at his and his pals' command.

The Daltons were already gone two days, and Charlie was feeling so much better under the careful nursing of his sister, who had strict orders to keep the whisky bottle away from him, that he was

thinking of joining the boys on the very next day, when, in the middle of the night and without any warning whatever, the whole force of Ransom Payne's posse surrounded Daisy Bryant's house.

The Indian male-servant, whom the fair widow had trained to be both deaf and dumb on all such occurrences, opened the door promptly at the first knocking of Payne, who always ventured at the head of his men in any such particularly dangerous occasion.

Obeying preconcerted orders, the officers invaded every room in the house almost at the same time, not indulging in any parleying whatever, but just taking possession, as they would have stormed a fort under fire.

In one room, already half-dressed and her hand on a Winchester she had had no time to use, Daisy Bryant was discovered and provisionally hand-cuffed.

In the garret, in a very ingeniously contrived retreat, which contained a shake-down and other such primitive conveniences, Charlie was pounced upon, also unprepared to resist so rapid an attack.

He was made a prisoner, and a squad being left in the house to prevent Daisy Bryant or her Indian

help from communicating with the outside, Charlie,
pretty tightly hand-cuffed, was placed in Ed Short's
charge and marched in prompt order as far as the
Henessey station of the Rock Island R. R., there
to await the passage of the next train. It had been
decided to have Charlie Bryant conveyed to
Guthrie by way of Caldwell, Arkansas City and,
down south, by the Santa Fe R. R. as far as the
capital of the Oklahoma Territory.

This memorable trip was undertaken August the
23d, 1891. While traveling over the Santa Fe, Ed
Short had gone to sit with his prisoner in the Express car, the messenger being an old friend of his.
The train having stopped at Enid, a way station,
some time in the afternoon, Ed Short felt like
straightening his legs by a little walk on the platform. The prisoner seemed quiet enough and had
been fairly cheerful the whole day, protesting his
innocence and making sure to be set free by the
first judge who would have cognizance of his case.

Still, in spite of appearances, the handcuffs had
not been removed, and when Ed Short stepped
down he placed his revolver in the messenger's
hands with a sign of warning. The Wells-Fargo
man was a fellow of little experience, and he had

failed to recognize the true nature of the brigand who sat so demurely a few feet from him. So, heedless of Ed Short's silent warning, he laid the revolver by his side on the floor and began arranging a few packages just delivered him by the station agent.

Quick as lightning, the prisoner lowered his two hands, tightly bound together, within reach of the revolver, and picking it up noiselessly, glared with shining eyes toward the open door.

Just at that minute, he espied Ed Short on his way back to the car. Bang! bang! went the revolver!

Hit in the breast, then again in the neck, Short staggered and cried out:

"I am done for!"

But his indomitable pluck did not forsake him in this horrible moment. With a hand already trembling with the approaching agony, he pulled out his second revolver, and once, twice, thrice, fired at the crouching form of his murderer.

Without a word, without even a gasp, Charlie Bryant tumbled headforemost out of the car—a dead man.

And rolling by his side, still clutching his revengeful weapon, poor Ed Short, faithful to his

trust even unto death, fell down, vomiting his life's blood.

Captor and captured had met together before their Maker's judgment throne.

CHAPTER V.

Poor Ed Short was dead, shot down in the most cruel and cowardly manner by the chief accomplice and pal of the Dalton brothers, Charlie Bryant, the sister of Bob's paramour, Daisy Bryant, the dashing Hennessey grass-widow. For a time, it seemed as if this deed of blood, followed, like a flash of lightning, by the murderer's death, would cow down the

indomitable spirit of this band of desperadoes and disrupt their criminal league.

Ransom Payne's efforts had been so far successful that he had unearthed the gang's principal refuge, captured one of the leading spirits among those brigands and caged the fascinating creature whose clever dodges were of so great a help to the Daltons' comfort and security.

In the task, one of his trusted lieutenants had fallen, faithful to the last; but this was one of the forfeits to be paid whenever risking one's life in the dangerous career of defender of the law.

And it seemed as if this heavy sacrifice of a noble, unselfish existence was to put an effectual stop to this era of extraordinary lawlessness the Daltons had inaugurated, in boastful imitation of their predecessors and kinsmen, the Jameses and Youngers.

For months after this eventful twenty-third of August, 1891, when this bloody drama took place in front of the Express car of the Santa Fe train, the country that had trembled under the criminal sway of the Daltons was left surprisingly undisturbed.

It seemed almost as if the earth had swallowed up the whole gang, consigning it doubtless to that place in the lower regions where it truly belonged.

8

The place near Hennessey had been closed up, and remained so, all through the winter of 1891-92 and the following spring, although Mistress Daisy Bryant had been released from custody, no clear case of receiving stolen goods or harboring outlaws having been established against her. Of course Charlie was an outlaw, and there were several true bills found against him by various grand juries. But then he was undoubtedly her brother and she would never have been convicted if brought to trial for hiding her own flesh and blood from the pursuing officers.

So the fair and wily creature went off scot free, but not unwatched, however; for Ransom Payne and the Logan county district attorney's office felt certain that she would be sure to establish, sooner or later, some communication with the vanished Bob Dalton, and had great hopes to thus be able to reach and secure the remaining members of the most successful criminal association the Southwest had known for years.

Mistress Daisy was, however, too much even for Ransom Payne's experienced and vigilant foresight. After apparently settling down to a life of thrifty labor, as a dressmaker, under the very eyes of her watchers, in the city of Guthrie, she, one cool morn-

ing in early April, 1892, disappeared as if by magic.
Not the faintest clue did she leave behind her, and
during the winter months her mode of life had displayed no mysterious features.

So far, therefore, the officers of the law stood
baffled. But the continued in activity of the gang con-
vinced them that they must have disbanded or settled
down in some populous eastern town, away from
those who knew too much about their past career.

The fact is that, in a cosy little house built by
some early settler who had soon tired of the lone-
some neighborhood, away in Greer county, that
section of the Indian Territory claimed both by
Texas and Oklahoma. Daisy Bryant had finally
joined her beloved Bob, who had been living there
in clover all winter long with his inseparable chum,
Emmet, and in the company of two other men who
counted among his most reckless pals, "Tom Evans"
and "Texas Jack."

They had received their supplies through trusted
friends, and had kept all along so quiet and undemonstrative in a locality far distant from railroads
or causeways, that the presence there of this small
colony of strangers was hardly known at the nearest
settlement, over twenty-five miles away.

The purpose of Bob in thus remaining in absolute inaction for so long a time was evidently twofold: He found it necessary to put to sleep the lynx-eyed watchfulness of his arch-enemy Ransom Payne, and he wanted to gather about him a phalanx of such redoutable fellows as would throw terror in every village of the territories and border states. These two objects—the first especially—could not be attained in a week or a month. Payne would keep up his posse a-going all over the country until far into the winter season, or as long as the funds would allow him. Then some other case would be placed in his charge and the Dalton gang cease to become his sole and foremost consideration. Then, and then only, would the time come to resume operation.

And to do so "with a startler" as a first move, was now the goal of Bob Dalton's insatiable ambition. The man's peculiar trait never was either cruelty or greed—so much we must be allowed to say in his favor. But an inordinate vanity ruled his every action, a vanity before which everything and everybody had to bow, and which would lead him to any amount of bloody work if it could be satisfied in no other way. To surpass the record of every

robber in this country and time, and in all countries and times, was the stubborn aim of Bob's every thought and action.

In death, if not in a prolonged and disastrous career of crime, the young desperado's insane ambition was to find itself satiated, for the Coffeyville tragedy may be counted among the most extraordinary dramas of the age.

Winter had gone, spring had gone, fields and trees were alive again with verdant vegetation, farm life had resumed its activity, and still nothing was heard of the Dalton gang. They were getting among the old stories, in that super-active Southwest where months do the work of, and count for, years.

But the warm breeze of June had hardly begun raising the dust upon the highways, when this startling news ran through the country, with the exaggerated details that are sure to be added in such cases:

"Another train hold-up! The Daltons are out again!"

And so it was. Bob's forces had gathered again, and played their old game for a third time.

Ransom Payne to the rescue! Your arch-enemies are in the field!

Singularly enough, the theater of this new and daring outrage was but a few miles distant from the scene of the one immediately preceding. Apparently satisfied that nowhere else could his gang find an easier escape, their crime once committed, Bob Dalton had selected the Red Rock station, in the Oklahoma Territory, and on the Sante Fe road, just twenty-six miles from Wharton, as the point where he and his pals would stop and pillage the south-bound express that steams past this small depot in the early part of the night.

The Fast Texas Express on the Atchison, Topeka & Santa Fe R. R. was due on Thursday night, the 2d of June, 1892, at 9:40 P. M., past the Red Rock station, but was not to stop there unless signaled to do so. The settlement there is unimportant, and the depot is used almost exclusively for the loading of cattle to be carried northward. Night trains have very seldom occasion to stop there, except to receive some instructions from the train dispatcher at either end of the section, announcing some change in the movement of the trains.

So when the engine slowed up in answer to the signal, there was immediately some alarm manifest among the crew and those of the passengers who

were somewnat familiar with similar experiences. Their worst fears were soon to prove true.

For hardly had the train slacked speed in front of the wooden shanty used as the depot of Red Rock station, than six masked men rushed silently toward the engineer and had him bring the train to a standstill, their Winchesters significantly pointed where they could do the most harm.

Then the usual tactics, which might be called "the Daltons' own," were faithfully followed. The engineer being kept under watch, some distance from the locomotive, his fireman was directed to take his pick-axe and smash the door of the Express car, which the messenger declined peremptorily to open. A few shots fired in the air were sufficient warning for the train hands and passengers to keep quiet and undemonstrative within the sleepers and cars, and the threatening and revolting oaths of the robber in command soon caused the Express safe to be opened and its contents revealed. They were not by any means satisfactory to the gang, who expected a very different kind of a haul. They hardly got two thousand dollars for their trouble, and swore their choicest curses when thus dis· appointed.

They did not feel though like facing the possible resistance of the passengers, and their plunder gathered, they ordered the engineer and fireman back to their engine, and firing a final volley, this time through the windows of the passenger cars and sleepers, they disappeared through the night.

For the third time the robbers had got away without a scratch. One more of their crimes, had proved as easy of execution as its predecessors. It was time indeed that something should be done.

Be it said to the credit of the railroad company and the territorial authorities, not an hour was lost before starting in pursuit of the daring brigands.

Before dawn of the next morning, Wednesday, the 3d of June, sixteen men, well mounted and armed to the teeth, commanded by the indefatigable and determined Ransom Payne, were in full chase of the desperadoes, and for a couple of days seemed on the point of tracking them to their retreat.

The place in Greer county was discovered and raided.

It was absolutely empty of its inhabitants, however, Mistress Daisy having made good her escape But the signs of long occupancy by the band were

easily detected and many valuable points collected by the shrewd U. S. Deputy Marshal.

After covering an immense amount of ground, in an amazingly short time, the posse had to be dismissed and a few select men only kept at work, in a more mysterious manner, tracking, to the best of their abilities, each of the men supposed to be associated with Bob, Grat and Emmet Dalton in the commission of those repeated outrages.

The trains crossing the territory were now guarded with jealous care, the least rumor of a possible hold-up sufficing for a number of armed men being taken on board and carried along for a long distance.

Thus it was hoped to discourage any further criminal attempt of the kind. And this proved correct enough—for just *forty-two days*, that is, from June the second to the memorable Thursday, the fourteenth of July, 1892.

CHAPTER VI.

THE FAMOUS M., K. & T. ROBBERY.—EIGHT BOLD OUT-
LAWS OVERCOME NINE ARMED DETECTIVES—THE
ROBBERY OF THE MISSOURI, KANSAS & TEXAS
TRAIN AT ADAIR SURPASSES ALL PREVIOUS REC-
ORDS—ARMED GUARDS DRIVEN BACK INTO
THEIR CAR AND THE BOOTY HAULED OFF IN
TRIUMPH—ONE MAN KILLED AND FOUR
OTHERS WOUNDED — NO ONE EXCEPT
THE EXPRESS OFFICIALS AND THE
OUTLAWS KNOW HOW MUCH MONEY
WAS TAKEN—AN EYE-WITNESS'
STARTLING TESTIMONY.

As was stated before, after weeks of persistent
and exhaustive researches following immediately upon the Wharton hold up, Ransom Payne, having
been placed in charge of other business, had to give
up, for the present, his favorite occupation of tracking the Daltons. He had made it hot for them dur-

ing the whole time he was instructed to continue on their trail, the capture of Charlie Bryant not being the least important of his exploits.

But now, for some reason or other, probably because a general feeling of security had succeeded months of bewildered apprehension, Payne had only accidently busied himself with the Dalton case, and it was more and more apparent that only his untiring vigilance and his determined, fearless attitude had kept the rascals at bay. He out of the way, their city friends notifying them of the fact, the Daltons' reckless spirit had again full sway.

The Red Rock hold-up was a success; and through the country a rumor ran like wild fire:

"The Daltons are about yet; they'll be heard of soon again."

The Indians, although generally friendly to a degree toward their suppliers of fiery liquids, the outlaws, and keeping mum, with national taciturnity, concerning their whereabouts, had been heard to say between themselves that the Missouri, Kansas & Texas railroad would be the next line attacked by the gang, and this very soon.

Finally the territorial police was notified that the Daltons were encamped at or near Pryor creek,

a petty station on the M., K. & T., located forty-five miles north of Muskogee, in the Oklahoma Territory, the stations between being but of very insignificant importance.

It was decided, therefore, to have every train on the main line carefully guarded by a special force of men until full information should be received as to the capture or dispersion of the gang.

This wholesome precaution proved to be absolutely useless, as there was indeed a wide and radical difference between the fellows comprising this troop of police and the sturdy, indomitable fellows Ransom Payne had led through perils innumerable.

Here are the details of this incredible, and, in many respects, highly farcical encounter.

Adair is a small and lonely station on the Cherokee division of the Missouri, Kansas & Texas railroad. It had been rumored for two weeks, as stated above, that the Daltons were encamped near there between the town and Pryor creek. On the evening of July 14, 1892, at about nine o'clock, the gang, more numerous than ever before—eight of them, bad men, heavily armed—came to town. They went right to the depot and proceeded to business.

Although some of the houses in the small settle-

BOB AND GRAT

The two Dalton Brothers Photographed after their Death

FRONT OF THE CONDON BANK, SHOWING MARKS OF THE FIGHT WITH THE DALTON GANG

ment were still lighted and people seen, grouped in friendly conversation, the men, carefully masked, entered the little station.

The depot agent, under menace of Winchesters, was made prisoner. Then the gang looted the place, taking all the money and valuables to be found. They bound the agent and put him in a corner.

This took but little time. The northbound train No. 2, the one which the men had come to rob, was not due until 9:45. So the eight robbers sat down on the platform and calmly waited for the train to come.

It was on time. When the engineer slowed up at the platform, there was a detachment of the eight waiting to claim the attention of Engineer Glen Ewing and his fireman.

They were both put under cover of Winchesters and were requested to keep quiet.

Others of the robbers formed a reception committee to greet Conductor George Scales and his porter when they stepped off the train, and they were made captives before they knew what was stirring.

In accordance with the Daltons' invariable cus-

tom, the fireman was told to come down out of the cab, and bring his coal pick along. He was conducted to the door of the Express car and ordered to make ready to smash it.

The messenger, George Williams, refused to open the door. One of the robbers announced in a loud voice that he had just put a big stick of dynamite under the car, and some of the others fired a few shots through the windows just to notify Messenger Williams of the extreme gravity of the situation. The door was opened.

In swarmed the greedy robbers with their guns aimed at the messenger. They made him unlock the safe and they pulled everything they could lay hands upon out of it and piled it upon the floor of the car. Then the three robbers in the car took away the messenger's watch, bound that unhappy wight and dumped him in an out of the way corner. From out of the darkness there appeared a spring wagon driven by one of the robbers. It backed up to the door and the heaped-up plunder was shoveled into it. Then the business-like Daltons prepared to depart.

It would doubtless interest the reader to know what kind of attitude was that of those valiant guards, carried free and well paid by the railroad

company for the special purpose of fighting and
bringing to bay those very brigands who had just
been looting the train they were in.

The nine good men and true, headed by a certain
J. J. Kinney, their worthy captain, had taken possession of the smoking car, and, surrounded by their
many weapons, announced to the admiring passengers that they were on their way to signal victory
over those —— —— scoundrels and brigands—the
Daltons.

Having stated their bloodthirsty intention and
looking every inch, in looks and costume, the twin
brothers of these very desperadoes they were sent to
meet, capture or kill, they proceeded "to imbibe"
and to exchange jocose and boasting remarks.

It was noticed, however, that the nearer the
northbound train No. 2 came to the notorious Pryor
creek, the quieter and visibly uneasier grew the
bellicose crowd.

But when Pryor creek was passed without un-
pleasantness, and also the next station, Perry, the
drooping spirits of the "brave" police revived marvelously, and a festive drink was absorbed in honor
of this narrow escape, which the men boisterously
qualified of "——bad luck."

Just seven minutes later—for Perry and Adair are but three and a half miles apart—the engine slacked speed and finally came to a full stop with something more than ordinary suddenness.

There was a rumor outside.

The train hands were noticed running about, lanterns on their arms.

The guards looked at each other in silent dismay, but not a son of them budged an inch. Talk had died on their lips, and so had whatever meager measure of courage they might have even possessed. Mice are not more discreet when they hear the steps of the housewife—

The chiefs, Captain Kinney and Captain La Flore, the latter a Cherokee half-breed and chief of the Cherokee Indians' special police force, stood up alone and began an animated but whispered conversation at the further end of the car.

"How many are there, do you think?" said Kinney

La Flore ventured his head out of the window, but brought it back in a hurry, for a regular salvo from the enemy's Winchesters was fired as a threatening warning.

"I saw seven of 'em," he whispered. "Might be a dozen more for what I—know."

"Well, boys," called out Kinney, feeling that the situation was growing critical, "shall we go out and fight them—?"

This singular way of commanding his men to do their duty met with the expected answer—that is, no answer at all. They were not going to hazard their precious skins, not they, and the captain had better understand it right away.

Still it would never do to reach the next station and have to acknowledge themselves such arrant cowards; so, about the time the robbery was all over, these guards consented to become dimly aware of what was going on, and, rising cautiously from their seats, they opened a rapid fire at the freebooters through the car windows. The robbers replied with promptness and much vigor. Bullets whistled everywhere. Somewhat emboldened now, and the two captains not being after all such absolutely despicable funks, a few of the guards followed their lead out of the smoking car down on the side of the track where the robbers were not and began shooting between the cars at the retreating forms of the bandits. Undaunted though and briskly firing back, the robbers, none of whom seemed to have been hit by the wild firing of their pusillanimous adversaries, loaded

their wagon and drove merrily off towards the woods, firing as they went.

After the robbers had disappeared in the dark, it was found that their fire had been deadly.

In a drug store near the depot Doctors W. L. Goff and Youngblood had been sitting comfortably, exchanging remarks about the day's work. The noise of the fight soon told them what the trouble was; a few stray bullets tore through the frame wall of the building and both of the men were struck by them.

Dr. Goff died in a short time.

Dr. Youngblood's condition was so serious that he was long at death's door.

The robbers' bullets wrought injury among the guards, too. Captain Kinney was slightly wounded in the shoulder and La Flore received a superficial wound on the arm, while a guard named Ward was slightly injured.

Thus was the honor of the Indian police saved from absolute and unredeemable ruin.

All this shooting created a great panic, of course, among the passengers, who were frightened almost into a frenzy. But none of them were harmed; the Daltons, as usual, confining themselves to express

safe pillaging whenever they went on a business tour.

As the reader may not feel like believing the whole of our positive statement concerning the extraordinary conduct of Captain J. J. Kinney's guards, we beg leave to insert herein the very words in which one of the passengers on board train No. 2 narrated the actual facts and stigmatized the fellows' behavior.

Mr. J. T. Hearn, of St. Louis, arrived on July 16th at Coates Hotel, Kansas City, from the Southwest, where he had been on a business trip. He was one of the passengers on the Missouri, Kansas & Texas train that was held up at Adair, I. T., on that eventful Thursday night. He was awake and witnessed the entire fight and has some very strong opinions about the detectives and Indian police on board the train. He characterized their conduct as cowardly in the extreme and deserving of universal condemnation. In speaking of the very exciting episode Mr. Hearn said:

"It was about 10 o'clock and every one in the sleeper had retired excepting myself. We were bowling along right merrily on the other side of Adair, and on stopping at that station I glanced out

of the window.   I saw some rather uncertain figures
and a wagon standing near.   Then came a few scat-
tering shots, and then the batch of detectives piled
out of the coaches.

"Inside of ten minutes there were no less than
200 shots exchanged and, during that time, the passengers were secreting their valuables or crouching
low to escape the rain of bullets from all sides.
Then the firing let up a little and the valiant detectives came tumbling in pellmell, any way to reach
shelter.   Chief Detective Kinney had a slight
wound in the fleshy part of the left arm.   There
seemed to be about fifteen of the detectives, and
early in the evening I had noticed them and re-
marked what fearless looking fellows they were.
Every one looked the typical "bad man" and they
were armed to the teeth.

"A passenger asked the chief if the men were
gone and he answered that they were in the express car.   Then some one asked why the detectives
were not outside trying to prevent the robbery, and
they made scant reply.   Several suggested that they
could waylay the robbers as they emerged from the
car, as by actual count there were only seven, or at
most eight of them; but the detectives only replied

by finding safe shelters behind the seats and on the rear platform. I had placed my watch and pocket-book under the edge of the carpet on the floor of the sleeper, but there were so many detectives on the floor that I thought the valuables would be safer in my pocket, so I returned them to their proper places.

"After awhile the robbers dumped all the stuff they wanted from the express car into the spring wagon, got up on the seats, and drove twice around the entire train, firing as they went. All the time the detectives were in their holes with the exception of one man about fifty-five years of age. He was fighting all the time until he received a wound in the shoulder from one bullet, while another plowed a furrow across his breast. Another man was shot through the left forearm, the bullet passing on and striking his watch. That stopped both the bullet and the timepiece. Afterward he laid the watch out on a piece of paper. It was in so many pieces that it could be gathered up and sifted through the fingers.

"A stray bullet struck a physician in a drug store up town, cutting an artery in the thigh. They thought when we left that he would bleed to death.

"That batch of detectives was on the train in the expectation of an attempt being made at robbery, and they were very brave until the time came for action."

DEAD CRIMINALS.

CHAPTER I.

RANSOM PAYNE TO THE RESCUE—POSSES AGGREGATING
OVER ONE HUNDRED MEN ORGANIZED BY THE BRAVE
UNITED STATES DEPUTY MARSHAL—HE LEADS THE
MOST DETERMINED BAND OF THE LAW'S DEFEND-
ERS—LARGE REWARDS OFFERED BY THE M., K.
& T.—THE BRIGANDS ARE TRACKED AND
FORCED TO DISPERSE—THE EL RENO BANK
OUTRAGE WRONGLY ASCRIBED TO THE
DALTONS—BOB'S PLANS FOR ROBBING
THE COFFEYVILLE BANKS MATUR-
ING—HIS NIGHT VISITS TO THE
CITY — DRUGGIST BENSON'S
STARTLING ADVENTURE.

The news of the Adair hold-up, the incredible
details about the cowardice displayed by the Indian
police, and the startlingly easy success of the Dal

tons' bold raid in the face of armed forces they must have known to be on board the northbound train of the M., K. & T., on that eventful Thursday, the 14th of July, 1892, caused an immense emotion all through the territories and the border states.

It seemed, indeed, as if there were no security left for railway passengers, and as if the moneys in transit were to be henceforth at the mercy of this reckless band of robbers.

The time had come for a gigantic effort that would wipe out this triumphant band of outlaws, and restore some tranquiilty to travelers and express companies.

Besides, the pitiful conduct of the Indian police showed but too clearly that the citizens would have to depend on themselves only and on their fearless efforts to protect the peace and good name of their region. A general cry came up from among all those who had kept posted concerning the criminal annals of the couple of years preceding, and it was:

"Call Ransom Payne and his men to the rescue!"

And the Missouri, Kansas & Texas R. R. caused it to be publicly announced that large rewards, aggregating six thousand dollars, would be paid for the

MISSOURI, KANSAS & TEXAS RAILWAY COMPANY.

Parsons Kas. — July 15th 1872

$ 5000 Reward!

The Express Car on the north bound train of the M.K. and T. Ry. was robbed by masked men at Adair, Indian Territory Thursday night July 14th. A Reward of Five Thousand Dollars will be paid by the undersigned for the Arrest and Conviction of each of the men engaged in this Robbery to an amount not exceeding Forty Thousand Dollars.

Signed { M.K. & T. Ry. Co.
by Alex C. Purdy.
Assen't Vice President.

{ Pacific Express Co.
by L.A. Fuller,
Superintendent.

capture and conviction of the robbers who had so successfully raided their northbound Express. We have picked up in one of the way stations of the company one of those hand-written posters, and we reproduce it here.

But the plucky and shrewd U. S. Deputy Marshal and the brave and true men gathered around him were this time to be the mainstay of pursuing justice, and it took but a few hours for the posses, three in number, and including over one hundred well-armed and determined men, to be set on the different trails left behind them by the Adair robbers.

For the Daltons and their pals had dispersed almost at once, not specially caring to attract by their number the attention of the settlements they would have to cross to reach their various destinations.

The wildest rumors concerning the lightning rapidity and secrecy with which Bob Dalton conducted his operations were now spreading all over the territory and the bordering Kansas towns, and every act of particularly bold outlawry was placed to his credit.

So it came to pass that hardly had the first emotion succeeding the Adair robbery died out when

robbers appeared in El Reno, on the Choctaw Coal and Railway Company's lines, one morning, and when the streets were crowded with people and teams entered the leading bank of the city.

The only person in the bank at the time was the wife of the president, who fainted at the first sight of the revolvers. The bandits leisurely took all the money in sight, and remounting their horses rode away. The raid netted them $10,000, which was such a severe loss to the bank that it was forced into liquidation.

To this day the raiders in this case were not discovered and it has always been the general, although probably erroneous opinion, that the Daltons tried their hands bank-robbing at the expense of this little Oklahoma community.

" I have no doubt," Superintendent C. H. Eppelsheimer, of the Pinkerton detective agency, said, in in an interview with a Kansas City reporter, " that many crimes have been laid at the doors of the Dalton boys that they were not guilty of. I am not defending them in the least, but in this respect they resembled the James boys. In their time every robbery and crime committed in this section was laid to them, while it is an unquestioned fact that they

knew nothing of many of the occurrences. So it
was with the Daltons."

We only mention this well worded opinion because we think it backed by facts, and also because
we earnestly believe that the first time the Dalton
gang ever attempted bank robbing was on the tragic
fifth of October, which our narrative is now approach·
ing.

For by that time, that is six weeks and over after
the Adair hold-up, the ground was indeed becoming
too hot for the boys.   The systematic search undertaken by Ransom Payne and his faithful followers,
the wholesome excitement generally spread all over
that region could not fail, within a very short time,
to end in the capture of the robbers.   The only
refuge left them was flight, disappearance, dispersion of the gang, and all this needed money, a good
deal of it, for Bob well knew that in other parts of
the country he would have to lay low for quite a
while until a new band could be formed and new
connections created that would facilitate his escape
after each criminal attempt.

And thus germinated in his mind the audacious
scheme of raiding some wealthy village bank, and
with the funds thus gathered in to vanish for a time,

THE FARMERS' HOME.

In the smallest building, at the left of the picture, lay the wounded Emmet Dalton, until he was taken by the sheriff to the County Jail, at Independence, Kansas.

away from his favorite stamping grounds, rendered so thoroughly uncomfortable by Ransom Payne's untiring and intelligent efforts.

That the name of Coffeyville was the first to come to him seems natural, considering that he had lived long enough in this vicinity to gain a thorough knowledge of the lay of the land, securing for his band, as he thought, an unnoticed access and an easy exit.

Besides, he had kept himself well posted about whatever changes had taken place in the prosperous little city, and since the event we are about narrating happened, it has been discovered that more than once had Bob, Grat and Emmet, either alone or separately, paid nightly visits to the place they had but a few years before, in the time of their honest youth, made their regular home.

The landlord of the queer little hostlery, the sketch of which is to be found in this little volume and which was called by the rather ambitious name of the *Farmer's Home*, told his friends,—since the destruction of the Dalton gang set his tongue free —that, more than once, had he been awakened in the dead of night by Bob knocking at his window. He had been forced, on those occasions, to admit

the robber chief and those of his men that were with him. The landlady had been called upon to prepare a warm supper for the "gentlemen of the highway," and to accept their thanks—instead of their money. At the time, the terror those precocious bandits inspired was such that there was no thought of refusing them anything, or any imprudent talking, the next day, over the incident.

But another visit of Bob within the precinct of Coffeyville took place, very shortly, in fact within the week preceding the famous raid of October 5th. It was curious enough to deserve a detailed account.

On Walnut street, just a few doors from the post-office, there exists a drug store conducted by Frank Benson, manager and partner of the firm of George Slosson & Co. About a week or ten days before the raid, a little before midnight, a man knocked a long while at the door of Mr. Benson's home for admission.

Awakened from his sleep, Mr. Benson cried out, "Who's there?"

The stranger replied, calling Mr. Benson by name and urging him to come down.

Another demand as to his identity was met as evasively, and, moved by the man's persistence, Mr.

Benson at length partially dressed himself and opened the front door, leaving the latched screen door between himself and his visitor.

There stood Bob Dalton, upon whose head a great price was set, a revolver in his hand, the pearl handle of another gleaming at his belt, filled round about with cartridges. Mr. Benson had not seen him for a great length of time, but he recognized him immediately.

Dalton threateningly demanded that Mr. Benson sell him a gallon of alcohol.

They don't care much for whisky down in the fire nations. They drink alcohol down there—a gallon of it will go as far as a barrel of whisky.

Benson said that he did not sell alcohol, that he had none in his store, and that the sale of it was against the law. Bob was not to be moved, though, from effecting a purchase or exacting a free gift, and he insisted that Benson go to his drug store and make the sale.

At length Benson managed to partly convince the outlaw of the truth of his statement and sent him off upon another track by directing him to Rammell Brothers, druggists, on the opposite side of the square, on Union street, next door to the First

National Bank, as a firm which kept alcohol in stock.

"Did he get it there?" Mr. Benson was, later asked by a reporter.

"I don't know whether he did or not."

When Mr. Benson closed and locked the door on the departing desperado, he felt a ton lighter. The longer he thought of the visit the luckier he felt himself to be.

Next day he confidentially told his friends of the visit he had received. He did not go publicly about proclaiming that Bob Dalton was in the neighborhood, for that would be an indiscretion that such outlaws as the men who now lie dead in their graves, in Coffeyville, frequently rebuked with knife and bullet with murderous promptitude.

Mr. Benson's friends could scarcely believe his statement. They did not doubt his integrity, but it seemed impossible that a man for whose capture so many thousands of dollars had been offered would dare to return to a locality where his identity was so generally known and where his capture would not be a matter of that bloody difficulty which attended pursuit of him in his fastnesses in the country.

10

So they mocked at Benson as a dreamer of idle things, as one who walked in his sleep and saw impossible visions, and as one fond of being the hero of imaginary adventures.

This brings us within tnese days of the great tragedy. Other sources of information, and especially the statements extracted from the wounded Emmet, furnish sufficient evidence as to the careful and business-like manner in which Bob Dalton had been preparing the great robbery that was to make him the most famous brigand of the age

CHAPTER II.

It is universally admitted that the extraordinarily bold attack upon the two banks of Coffeyville, Kan., that took place, in broad daylight, on Wednesday morning the 5th of October, 1892, that the thrilling fight, the courage displayed alike by bandits and citizens, make up the most wonderful story the border has ever furnished. Such a chapter of western life has not been written since the romance went out of the rough riding, bank robbing,

train wrecking career of the James boys and the Youngers in that disastrous raid of the Minnesota village of Northfield.

Probably the easily gotten wealth obtained from the express car of the northbound train of the M., K. & T. R. R., on the 14th of July, took swift wings; probably the delights of easy moving circles of Denison and Fort Smith, where it is said the members of the hunted Dalton gang disported themselves even under the federal eye were expensive. More probably yet, the necessity of escaping, by an immediate exile from their usual haunts, the close hunt of the persistent, indefatigable Ransom Payne, made itself more strongly apparent day after day. Whatever may have moved the band to fresh action, certain it is that when some two weeks ago Emmet Dalton was working on a ranch twenty miles south of Tulsa, in the territory, he received a letter sent by his daring brother Bob from his safe point of hiding in the nation. Bob wrote that he had found a plan of profitable action on lines of endeavor quite distinct from those which had heretofore engaged his professional attention; would Emmet join him?

Emmet answered the letter in person. Where

that place of rendezvous may have been he refuses to tell. His statement speaks of a fortuitous meeting between him and Bob, but denies all regular, preconcerted appointment. Doubtless there are yet, in that lair, spoils well worth the hiding.

With Bob Dalton were the men who aided him in the train robbery on the Missouri, Kansas & Texas at Adair. There was Grat Dalton, whose life sat so lightly upon his consciousness that he was fattening out of the recollection of men who knew him a year before. There was Dick Broadwell, whose father lives in Hutchinson, Kan., and who had become so experienced a desperado in so astonishingly short a time that men thought "Texas Jack" was with the gang; finally there was Bill Powers, of the Three D ranch, the equal in daring of that Tom Hedde whom Coffeyville took him to be. Bob Dalton's plan, when unfolded to his youthful brother from the Tulsa ranch, was the robbing of the Coffeyville banks, but both of them at the same time, an exploit amazing enough to throw in the shade the most famed raids of Jesse James, the Youngers and their imitators.

In Coffeyville, as we narrated at some length, the Daltons had long lived. There, in the Daltons,

lot in the cemetery, lay buried Dalton, the father, a man of gruff disposition, but whose laziness and love of ease smothered a viciousness which lacked determination to become assertive. There, too, was buried Frank Dalton, a brother, who died a U. S. deputy Marshal in 1889; when across the Arkansas from Fort Smith he pumped his Winchester valiantly to the last, fighting criminals against great odds. Every by path and road in the country hereabout the surviving Dalton brothers knew minutely, every place of concealment, every avenue of escape; the people of the town and the neighborhood they were also fully acquainted with, for their last stay was but three years old.

Bob Dalton formed the plan, and the others accepted it without question.

Later, when interrogated, Emmet Dalton, then lying upon a bed he probably thought his death-bed, made a long rambling statement which our readers will find given in full in these pages and which contains the following lines, easily explained when one remembers that the wounded brigand thought himself about to be lynched by the infuriated population:

"When Bob explained his plans to me, saying that he could discount the James boys and rob two

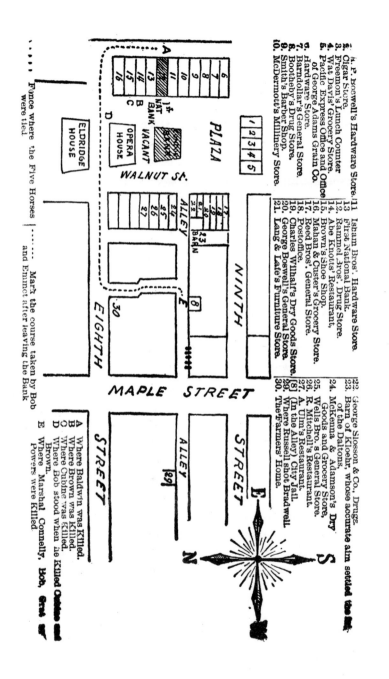

banks in a day, and adding that they were going to do it, right here in Coffeyville, *I tried to prevail on the boys not to come up,* for the people here had done us no harm; but finally I had to join for love of my brothers and because I had no money to get out of the country on, and was sure to be chased just as hard whether I joined or not."

Whether the protest of Emmet against the proposed raid was entered or not, nobody shall ever know. He fell in line, this is sure, and the same night camped with *the boys* not far from the Davis farm, in the Onion creek bottoms. The next morning, Wednesday the fifth, the gang rode to the conquest of the Coffeyville banks.

The horses, it appears, all belonged to Bob, evidently the treasurer as well as the president of this unholy association, and several had been bought on purpose for this raid.

Between 9:30 and 10 o'clock on that Wednesday morning, as Mr. and Mrs. R. H. Hollingsworth were driving west on what is known as Eighth street (see our Diagram of the Coffeyville Business Center), they met six mounted men at a point two hundred yards east of the old cheese factory, and less than half a mile from the western limits of the city

They were both attracted to the men by the peculiar appearance of the party, and the fact that they were all heavily armed. They agreed that there were six men and six horses in the party.

Within a hundred yards east of where they passed Mr. and Mrs. Hollingsworth, the same party was met by Messrs. J. M. and J. L. Seldomridge, who were driving west on the same road. They, too, were attracted by the appearance of the riders, and were led to remark that the men were undoubtedly on some strange mission, as they were armed to the teeth and apparently disguised. These gentlemen are also firm in their declarations that the crowd consisted of six persons and the same number of horses. Persons residing on Eighth street, east of what is known as the Hickman property, saw the party pass their residences. Of the large number of other people who observed this troop of horse-men, every one, however, asserts that there were only *five* riders in the party when they passed over that thoroughfare. They were seen by parties all along the street up to where Maple street crosses Eighth, and no one counted more than five horsemen. It is presumed that one of the party either backed out as they were about to enter town, or else diverged his

course into a cross street and made a circuit through
the southwestern portion of the city, in order to
reach the plaza from the south and aid in stamped-
ing the citizens from that point in case of an attack.

Anyhow, he was never seen since met by the
Hollingsworths and Seldomridges.

The five men rode boldly and at a swinging trot,
raising a cloud of dust which literally enveloped
them as they passed down Eighth street. They
turned into Maple street and passed alongside of
the Long-Bell Company's office and entered the alley that runs from Walnut street, at Slosson's drug
store, to Maple street and thence to the western
boundary of the city.

There were a number of persons in the alley at
the time and several teams were hitched in the rear
of Davis' blacksmith shop. An oil tank of the Con-
solidated Company, with two horses attached thereto,
was standing near McKenna & Adamson's stables,
almost in the center of the alley.

The party hitched their horses to the fence in the
rear of Police Judge Munn's lot, and within a few
feet of the temporary residence which he is at present occupying. [See Diagram.] A stone-cutter,
who was examining some rock lying near the city

ARRIVAL OF THE DALTON GANG AT COFFEYVILLE.—PAGE 155.

jail, observed them riding into the alley and dismounting.

All of the robbers were cleanly shaven except
Powers, who retained his heavy, dark brown moustache; Emmet, who could not sacrifice the down
upon his young lip; and Grat, who kept his scraggly
little moustache. No one knows whose razor went
over those five faces within two hours of the raid.

Dismounting from their horses, Bob and Grat
Dalton and Dick Broadwell ineffectually disguised
themselves with black beards. Meanwhile the town
rested unconscious of their coming and unprepared
for the attack. There had been some talk of the
possibility of a raid, as there had been in all the
towns along the border, but such unconcerted prep-
aration as may then have been made to meet such
an emergency had been quite forgotten

The desperadoes had quickly formed into a sort
of military line, three in front and two in the rear,
and walked closely together. The stone-cutter mentioned above walked closely in the rear of the crowd
as they passed from their horses through the alley,
until they reached the street, when he turned north
to his work at the other end of the block.

The alley opens upon the public square about

THE DESPERADOES ENTERING THE CONDON BANK.

which is clustered the whole business of the thriving
town directly in line with Condon's bank and almost
directly across the street from the First National
bank.   The robbers came out on the street in a close
bunch at a dog trot, their Winchesters hanging in
their arms ready for use.   Alex McKenna stood on
the steps of his store at the alley's mouth.

"There goes the Daltons," he said, in alarm.
Black beards hid no identities from McKenna's
eyes, but there was no wish in McKenna at that
moment to make himself conspicuous.

After silently passing Alex McKenna's store
the men quickened their pace and three of them
went into C. M. Condon & Co.'s bank at the southwest door, while the two in the rear ran directly
across the street to the First National bank, and entered the front door of that institution.   The next
thing that greeted Mr. McKenna's eyes was a Winchester in the hands of one of the men, and pointed
toward the cashier's counter in the bank.   He realized the situation at once, and called out to those in
the store, that "the bank was being robbed."

The cry was taken up by some others who had
been attracted to the men as they entered the bank,
and quickly passed from lip to lip all around the

square. Persons in the south part of the plaza, the open space between Walnut street and Union street, could plainly see the men as they moved around through the bank.

The two men who entered the First National bank were observed by a number of parties, but their presence did not attract any particular attentention at first.

The scenes that took place in the two banks were wonderfully exciting and must be described in detail in order to be understood.

CHAPTER III.

ROBBING TWO BANKS IN ONE DAY—THE GREATEST FEAT
OF THE KIND EVER ATTEMPTED—GRATTAN HEADS
THE PARTY TO THE CONDON BANK—THE CASHIER'S
MARVELOUS PRESENCE OF MIND—THREE MINUTES
GAINED SAVED THE BANK—BOB AND EMMET
RAID THE FIRST NATIONAL—$20,000 STOWED
IN A BAG—COOL AND COLLECTED, BOTH
PARTIES BEGIN THEIR RETREAT
LADEN WITH SPOILS.

—————

The five robbers now reached the door of the Condon bank. Emmet and Bob stood without and for a minute or so, lent the tenor of their silent presence. The others went within. There behind the counters, with interposing panels of glass and wickets of brass, were Charles Ball, the cashier, with brains in his head, and Charles Carpenter, one of the proprietors of the bank.

In the safe in the vault was $18,000.

Grat Dalton addressed himself at once to busi-

ness. Broadwell took his stand at one door and Powers at the other. With oaths and threats they demanded that the cashier place all the bank's money in a two-bushel wheat sack, which was produced, and fingers trifled with triggers with menacing carelessness.

"The time-lock doesn't go off until 9:45 o'clock," said the cashier, blandly conscious the while that the safe stood unlocked.

As he spoke, there was across the street short, fat, gray-bearded John D. Levan, the money loaner,

There was no stranger in sight as he crossed the street from the west. Emmet and Bob Dalton had passed over to the First National bank when they saw the Condon bank officials caged. He had heard that the Daltons were coming, and he meant to warn the bankers. He opened the door, and as he did so his arm was grasped by a muscular hand, and he was jerked prisoner within.

"The time-lock doesn't go off until 9:45 o'clock?" said Grat Dalton, interrogatively, as he looked at a gold watch, which was the souvenir of some gay exploit, and then he swore famously.

"Well, time'll be up in three minutes; we'll wait."

Those three minutes cost the members of the Dalton gang their lives and treasure. The men of the town awoke in that length of time to action. The delay was fatal, and it was the lie of the quick-witted cashier which occasioned it.

Dry Goods Clerk James leisurely crossed the street. He had a draft to be cashed, and his mind was on ribbons, not robbers. Like Levan, he, too, opened the bank door, and he, too, was grasped as he entered and held prisoner at the Winchester's muzzle, but the robbers did not fail to improve the three minutes' wait to the utmost. They compelled Cashier Ball to put in the bag all the currency in the drawer. Some three thousand dollars in silver they rejected as weighty and useless.

And they were men of business, these robbers.

"How much cash did the books show to be on hand the night before at the close of business?"

"Four thousand dollars," said the cashier, making little of the eighteen thousand dollars in the safe. "The money for the day's business will come later by express," he explained agreeably.

Luther Perkins, the capitalist, who owns the bank building, hearing the noise below and seeing from his window armed men enter the First National

bank across the street, took a pistol in each hand
and went down the back stairway. There he opened
the rear door of the Condon bank and Broadwell
had his Winchester upon him before he could move
a step. Mr. Perkins could fairly see the ball moving toward him, and shutting the door hastily re-
treated with his pistols up the stairway to his office.

There was hurrying about of men from store to
store in search of arms and confused preparations
for attack on all sides of the square, and before the
expiration of that three minutes wait it was learned
that the Dalton gang was at work in both banks.

On the east side Iceman Cyrus Lee spread the
alarm. He was on his wagon in front of the First
National bank when Emmet and Bob Dalton passed
before him and entered the money changer's house.
Despite a false beard he knew Bob at once. He
jumped from his wagon and rushed into Isham's
hardware store, next door to the bank.

"The Daltons are robbing the bank!" he cried,
and Cattle Dealer J. H. Wilcox knew the robber,
too, and called out from his office above the Condon bank. Folks in the stores laughed at Lee, but,
nevertheless, he ran with his warning to every store
on the east side of the square.

Just as he reached the south end of the block, Harness Maker Miller opened fire on the robbers in the Condon bank with his Winchester.

After the first shot he gained a station on top of the awning and pumped bullets quickly through the window of the bank eighty yards away. The first shot pierced the plate-glass window front and slightly wounded Broadwell.

" I'm shot," he said composedly, and then patronizingly suggested to Ball and Carpenter that they go into hiding under the counter, "or else you will get killed by some of these people," he added.

Miller was joined by others in the attack. The patter of bullets became a shower and then a storm; but the desperadoes bided their time and made no present attempt to fight or flee, though bullets hustled in from all parts of the square before them.

Meanwhile all went well with Bob and Emmet Dalton, and their visit at the First National bank had proceeded most favorably, as far as *their* interests were concerned.

When the two men entered the bank, Cashier Thomas G. Ayers and W. H. Shepherd, the teller, were in the front room behind the counter, and J. H. Brewster was transacting business with the former.

They covered all three of these gentlemen with their Winchesters, and addressing Mr. Ayers by name, directed him to hand over all the money in the bank.

At the same time one of the men, keeping his Winchester at ready command, ran into the back room and drove Bert S. Ayers, the bookkeeper, into the front part of the building where the vault is located.

Cashier Ayers very deliberately handed over the currency and gold on the counter, making as many deliveries as possible, in order to secure delay in hope of help arriving.

The bandit then ordered Mr. Ayers to bring out the money that was in the vault.

The cashier brought forth a package containing $5,000 and handed that over. About this time the fellow who was behind the counter discovered where the money was located, and proceeded to help himself to the contents of the burglar-proof chest, all of which, together with the money taken by the first burglar, were stuffed in a common grain sack and carefully tied up.

They then undertook to put the three bankers out at the front door, but a shot from the outside,

just as Mr. Ayers reached the pavement, evidently changed their plans, for the terrible fusillade of lead which swept up the square, made sheer madness any attempt to cross it in safety to their horses in the alley beyond.

Bob and Emmet accordingly turned and went out of the rear entrance of the bank, intending to go north in the alley to the first street, upon which the engine house fronts, then west to the business houses fronting the square from that direction, and then unperceived south to their horses in the alley.

The Ayers, father and son, and Shepherd they let go.

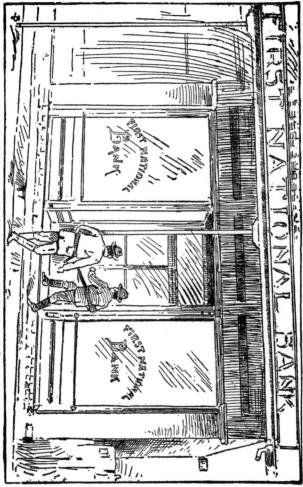

BOB AND EMMET DALTON ENTERING THE FIRST NATIONAL BANK

CHAPTER IV.

THE GREAT COFFEYVILLE TRAGEDY—THE DALTONS' LAST
FIGHT—HOW THE WAIT OF THREE MINUTES PROVED A
FATAL ONE—FEARFUL EXHIBITION OF BOB DAL-
TON'S SKILL WITH THE RIFLE—HIS DEADLY AIM
ACCOUNTABLE FOR THREE DEATHS—ONLY
THE QUICKNESS OF BRAVE JOHN KLOEHR
SUCCEEDS IN OVERPOWERING HIM—A
TOTAL OF FOUR CITIZENS KILLED AND
THREE WOUNDED—THE DESPERA-
DOES CLING TO THEIR BOOTY TO
THE VERY LAST—EMMET DAL-
TON'S LOVE FOR HIS BROTH-
ER CAUSES HIM TO BE
CAPTURED, WOUNDED
ALMOST TO DEATH—
BROADWELL FOUND
DYING ON THE
ROAD.

———

The noise of the first shot had brought every
man in the business center of the city into immediate
action.

From every advantage point a rifle or pistol sent lead hurling at the robbers now caged in the Condon bank, but Bob and Emmet Dalton were not forgotten.

It had been their plan, as the wounded Emmet confessed, to rob the banks without losing or killing a man.

" Bob wanted to show Coffeyville what he could do," gasped Emmet in explanation—and he did.

The brother desperadoes had no sooner gained the alley than they met Lucius M. Baldwin, a twenty-two-year-old clerk, whose widowed mother lives in Burlington, Kan. Baldwin had gone to Isham's hardware store at the first alarm and there snatched up a pistol, for all the hardware dealers of the city made free to all comers their stocks of firearms.

Baldwin hastily ran through the store, out in the alley behind, with the intent to take the Daltons in the rear.

One of the robbers ordered him to stop, but Baldwin, as he stated in his dying moments, did not hear the command, and mistaking the parties for men who were guarding the bank, continued to advance toward them.

Just then one of the robbers drew up his Win-

chester and exclaiming, "I have got to get that man," fired. The ball entered Mr. Baldwin's left breast, just below the heart, and he fell dying on the spot.

Several persons who were in the alley without arms, seeing the condition of affairs, took refuge in an adjoining building, while the men ran northward in the alley to Eighth street and thence west to Union street near Mahan & Custer's store, the one with the sack keeping in front of the other, the latter carrying his Winchester at a ready.

Bob's plan of escape was working well so far.

Quickly ejecting the shell, Bob joined his brother Emmet in a run and they soon gained the north end of the alley, the rattle of firearms in the square lending their heels swiftness.

Going west they ran in the center of the street upon which the Eldridge house is built and looking south. When they reached the square they saw up and down its sidewalks hastily armed men pouring lead into the Condon bank in a noisy stream. They hoped to cross unseen, and might have done so had it not been for the awaking within their breasts of the irresistible instinct to kill.

George Cubine, who worked in the shoe-shop of

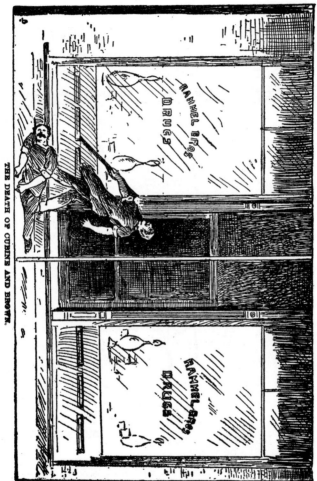

THE DEATH OF CUBINE AND BROWN.

D. W. Cubine, his uncle, near the northeast corner
of the square, pistol in hand, stood in the walk in
front of Rammel Bros.' drug store looking south in
the direction of the entrance to the First National

GEORGE CUBINE, ONE OF THE COFFEYVILLE HEROES.

bank, awaiting the exit of the robbers, whom he
supposed to be within.

By the side of Cubine, who had in old days been
a personal friend of the Dalton brothers, stood un-

armed Charles Brown, a fellow shoemaker and an old, harmless man. Cubine's back was turned to the Daltons, but Bob could not resist the temptation to stop in his unperceived flight and shoot.

CHARLES BROWN, ONE OF THE COFFEYVILLE HEROES.

Straight from his Winchester flew the bullet to Cubine's heart, and the man dropped dead on the walk.

Brown stooped to pick up the revolver from his companion's nerveless hand, and straightened his body and there whistled another bullet from that same deadly Winchester, and prostrate on one dead body fell another.

Bob Dalton's aim was fatally unerring and he needed never to shoot twice. The delay, though short as it was, cost him a moment of time and drew on him the attention of the citizens which had chiefly been directed to the robbers in the Condon bank.

As soon as Cashier Ayers, Bert Ayers and Shepherd found themselves in the street, driven out of the bank by the robbers, they ran into Isham's store adjoining. There the cashier caught a rifle from the hands of a man whom he remembers not, and just as the two Daltons ran across the street, north, he caught sight of them from the door of the store.

At that very minute poor Cubine fell mortally wounded, followed almost instantly by old man Brown. Seeing this, Cashier Ayers knelt to shoot, that he might shoot more accurately. He was within the door and almost hidden from observation by articles exposed for sale.

But Bob Dalton's quick eye spied him out—the

only thing in all that multitude of things that flashed in general view, hidden behind a wheel and harness, yet Dalton saw the head above the concealed body. The distance was fully seventy yards. Ayers had already aimed, yet in an inappreciable space of time that deadly Winchester came to the villain's shoulder and Ayers fell forward helplessly on the floor, a bullet in his head, his unused rifle in his sprawling hand. Blood spurted from the wound as if from a fountain.

Dalton laughed, and with his brother ran westward to the rear of the buildings, which there face the square, and turning to the south they ran to the alley, where their horses were tied, Bob Dalton carrying on his arm the sack which held the stolen treasure.

Meanwhile, the three desperadoes in Condon's bank had kept silent, though the fire was terrific. With dogged tenacity they were waiting for the expiration of the time which the cashier said the time lock had been fixed for.

Dalton's first rifle shot was to them the signal for escape. Boldly they prepared to sally out with such money as they had. All the town was firing at these robbers behind the plate-glass windows.

As soon as the shooting had begun, Liveryman John Kloehr, the best shot of the town, seeking a rifle, was given one by Barndollar from his own store. Gun in hand, he crossed to the southwest corner of the square and opened fire.

To silence the general fire and escape under cover of the confusion, through the plate glass windows the outlaws sent bullets back.

Boyish Harry Lang, Undertaker Lang's son, on the east side of the square near the alley, had a shotgun loaded with bird shot. He offered it to a man who declined to shoot when he was told what the gun was loaded with, whereupon the boy himself joined in the general conflict, although his bird shot merely flattened on the plate-glass window.

The storm of bullets raged heavily, and twenty bullet holes in the windows and their casings attest the vigor of it.

With a shout the three outlaws ran from the entrance, and Powers caught sight of Charlie Gump, a laborer, with a pistol in hand. Crack went his Winchester; the pistol dropped, and a hole in Gump's wrist marked the bullet's course.

That in the hail of bullets which then swept up the square all the flying robbers, who ran toward the

COFFEYVILLE CITIZENS SHOOTING AT THE GANG FROM ISHAM'S STORE.

alley where their horses were, were not killed seems miraculous.

A squad of men was gathered on the porch in front of Isham's store, from whence across the square, to and up the alley to where the horses stood, the field was clear. Volley after volley chased the fugitives. Mat Reynolds fired at one squad and wounded Powers. The man turned in his flight, made a face at Reynolds and returned the fire, wounding him in the foot. Joe Uncapper, from above the bank, wounded Broadwell with a bullet, but the man kept on and ran up the alley.

Bob and Emmet Dalton, approaching from the north in the rear of the business block facing the square, met Grat Dalton and his associates just as they all reached the barn where stood their horses. From the east up the alley came the flight of bullets, but they paid little heed. Bob Dalton tied the stolen $20,000 to the pommel of his saddle and said:

"We've got the swag, boys, and we'll keep it;" but the attack came closer. The squad on Isham's porch across the square kept their Winchesters hot.

John Kloehr, running to the south of the block on the west side of the square, passed through his

stable and came out behind a board fence on the alley, not fifty feet from where the Dalton gang came together.

Marshal Charles T. Connelly, taking the same course, had borrowed a rifle from Swisher's gun shop and came out upon the alley west of the robbers. He ran boldly out, looking westward and ignorant of the fact that the desperadoes were not fifty feet behind himself and Police Judge Charles Munn.

Grat Dalton raised his rifle, though wounded himself at the time with a bullet, and Connelly dropped dead with a bullet in his breast. Then Grat wheeled about to face the increasing storm.

The firing was so brisk that the outlaws did not dare to mount their horses and attempt escape. Bill Powers shot and killed two horses attached to an oil tank because their plunging disturbed his aim.

From his position behind the fence near by Kloehr took aim at Bob Dalton, just as he was ejecting a shell. Dalton caught sight of him and worked with such incredible rapidity that when he fell with a bullet from Kloehr's rifle in his bowels he discharged his reloaded gun. The bullet sped harm-

lessly in the air.   There was a convulsive motion and Bob Dalton was dead.

Grat Dalton caught sight of the assailant behind the thin fence. He lifted his rifle, but again Kloehr's Winchester spoke first and Grat Dalton fell dead with a bullet hole exactly in the center of his throat.

Emmet Dalton jumped to the saddle on Red Buck, his big bay racer, and transferred the money to his saddle. Bill Powers tried to mount his horse, when a shot from the squad on Isham's porch caught him in the breast, and tossing his gun up with a convulsive motion he fell dead near his leader.

Dick Broadwell reached his saddle in safety and led Emmet Dalton in the race for the western end of the alley.   A hail of bullets flew up the narrow alleyway. Broadwell reeled and blood spurted from his mouth, but he kept his saddle, crossed Maple street, and spurred his horse toward safety.

Then Emmet Dalton, boy as he was, with the down of his twentieth year on his lip to mark his youth, did as incredible a thing as men ever looked upon.

He reined his horse in before he had reached the exit from the alley, and in all that terrible, constant

CITY MARSHAL CHARLES T. CONNELLY.
The Dead Coffeyville Hero.

fire which fed the narrow crossway with leaden bullets, he deliberately rode back the whole distance to
where his brother Bob lay dead, dismounted and
tried to lift him upon the saddle of his horse that he
might bear him away.

A bullet from a Winchester shattered his right
arm near the shoulder, making a mere mass of
splinters of the bone.

Bob's body dropped and Emmet, holding the
rein as best he could, sought to use his left hand.
A load of buckshot struck him in the back and side.
Carey Seaman, a barber, fired the shot. When Har-
ris Reed told him, "of course that's one of the robbers, let him have it," there was a flash, a flame, a
cloud of smoke, and Emmet Dalton fell uncon-
sciously by the side of his brother, his arm shattered, his thigh broken, and a dozen buckshot in his
back.

Dick Broadwell rode on and on into the country
half conscious, bleeding from a dozen wounds and
swaying in his saddle. The direction of his flight
was soon discovered. A mounted posse gave chase.
A mile from the scene of the fight, near the gate
of the creamery on the Independence road, they
found him dead on the roadside, the bridle of his

EMMET DALTON, UNDER FIRE, TRYING TO SAVE HIS BROTHER BOB.

mounted horse in hand. How he came to his death is told in the following chapter.

We desire to state here, in order to contradict some unfounded reports that have been sent out by excited newspaper correspondents to the effect that the citizens were prepared for the attack, that when the robbers were discovered in the bank, there was not a single, solitary armed man anywhere upon the square or in the neighborhood.

Even Marshal Connelly had lain his pistol aside, and was totally unarmed when the alarm was given. Every gun that was used, with the exception of that brought into action by George Cubine, was procured in the hardware stores and loaded and brought into play under the pressure of the great exigency that was upon the people.

The firing was rapid and incessant for about three minutes, when the cry went up: "They are all down."

In an instant the firing ceased. Several men who had been pressing close after the robbers sprang into the alley, and covering them with their guns ordered them to hold up their hands.

One hand went up in a feeble manner.

Three of the robbers were dead and the fourth helpless.

Between the bodies of two of the dead highway-men, lying upon his face, in the last agonies of death, was Marshal Charles T. Connelly, the bravest of all the brave men who had joined in resisting the terrible raiders in their attempt to rob the banks.

Dead and dying horses and smoking Winchesters on the ground added to the horrors of the scene.

It took but a few minutes to discover who the desperadoes were. Tearing the disguises from their faces, the ghastly features of Grattan Dalton and Bob Dalton, former residents of Coffeyville and well known to many of our citizens, were revealed. The other dead body proved to be that of Bill Powers, whilst the wounded man was Emmet Dalton, the youngest brother of the two principals of the notorious gang.

The wildest excitement prevailed. Marshal Connelly breathed a few moments, when his brave spirit went out without a struggle. Emmet Dalton was carried to Slosson's drug store, and subsequently to Dr. Wells' office. At first he denied his identity, but realizing that he was recognized and likely to die, he admitted that he was Emmet Dalton.

It is simply impossible to describe the scenes

that followed. Excited men, weeping women and
screaming children thronged the square.

A few cool-headed citizens kept disorder from
ensuing. The dead and dying citizens were removed to their homes or other comfortable loca-
tions. The dead raiders' bodies were thrown into
the city jail. Guards were thrown out, and the city
sat down in sackcloth and ashes, to mourn for the
heroic men who had given their lives for the protection of the property of their fellow-citizens and
the maintenance of law in their midst.

CHAPTER V.

AFTER THE FIGHT—MOURNING FOR THE DEAD—THOU-
SANDS OF VISITORS POURING INTO THE CITY—MORE
DETAILS ABOUT THE KILLED DESPERADOES—YOUNG
T. N. RUSSEL THE SLAYER OF BROADWELL—THE
GHASTLY SIGHT WITHIN THE CITY JAIL—BURY-
ING THE BANDITS IN THE POTTER'S FIELD
—TALK OF LYNCHING EMMET NOBLY SUB-
DUED—THE CITIZEN-HEROES COMMIT-
TED TO THEIR GRAVES—THE DALTON
FAMILY ARRIVES—ALSO BROAD-
WELL'S RELATIVES—A TRUST-
WORTHY STATEMENT FROM
THE LIPS OF EMMET DALTON
—THE WOUNDED ROBBER
OFF TO INDEPENDENCE
UNDER CLOSE GUARD.

———

The smoke of the terrific battle with the bandits had blown aside, but the excitement occasioned by the wonderful event soon increased, until it reached fever heat.

The trains over the four principal roads leading to Coffeyville brought thousands of visitors to the scene of that bloody conflict between a desperate and notorious gang of experienced highwaymen and a brave and determined lot of citizens, who had the nerve to preserve their rights and protect their property under the most trying circumstances.

Shortly after twelve o'clock, noon, on that eventful Wednesday, that is, as soon as the telegraph had carried the news over to Parsons, Supt. Frey, of the M., K. & T., at the head of fifty heavily armed men, came down on a special train that ran over the thirty-one miles between Parsons and Coffeyville, in thirty-two minutes. When they reached their destination, however, they found that the brave little city had, unaided and alone, conquered and laid in the dust its criminal invaders.

Telegrams and letters offering assistance and extending condolence to the four stricken and bereaved families were received in great numbers from all parts of the country.

Those of the citizens who were not in the fight felt justly proud of those who were, and the latter meekly bore their laurels and assisted in restoring order and preserving the peace.

CAREY SEAMAN.

The heroic barber who shot down Emmet Dalton.

By comparing watches, it was discovered that less than fifteen minutes had elapsed from the time the Dalton boys entered the banks until four of their party were dead and the remaining one grievously wounded and in the hands of the officers.

Not over fifteen guns were actively engaged in the fight on both sides and the engagement lasted about ten minutes. Eight persons were killed and three wounded. The percentage of loss was greater than in any battle of the great war of the rebellion.

There were no "stray shots," either, no "accidental shootings." The fellows who held the guns were cool and collected.

The citizens of Coffeyville who were killed in the terrible engagement were each one engaged in the fight, and were not innocent bystanders. They are quiet and steady people in those southwestern border towns, but they are also adepts in the business of resisting law-breakers, and they know how to do their duty, though it costs blood.

The true inwardness of Broadwell's slaying was only fully revealed later in the day. It gave a new proof of the courageous blood that runs through the veins of the Coffeyville citizens, young and old, and it places on the roster of honor one more name, be-

T. N. RUSSELL.
The brave lad who shot the fleeing Broadwell.

sides those of the dead heroes, Connelly, Baldwin, Cubine and Brown; of the wounded ones, Gump, Reynolds and Dietz; and of those who escaped unscathed, John Kloehr and Carey Seaman first and foremost. This name is that of young T. N. Russell, whose experience, related by himself and corroborated by several eye witnesses, has its legitimate place in these pages.

It appears that when Broadwell—the only one of the desperadoes who managed to leave the fated alley, astride of his horse—rode on at the top of his mount's speed toward safety, he had to pass the back of G. W. Russell's lot, on the same alley, west of Maple street.

Just at that moment, the young son of Mr. Russell had run to the fence, a heavy Colt revolver in his hand, intent upon doing his share in the fight that was raging but a few yards away.

He espied the rider rushing toward him, urging his horse like mad and flourishing his trusty Winchester; and as the man passed him, not five feet distant, the lad let go his revolver, once, twice, thrice—

The robber uttered a yell as if touched in a vital part, but continuing his break-neck riding, contenting himself with discharging his Winchester behind his back, without even turning his head.

Not half a mile farther, the pursuing posse found him dead on the roadside, still holding the bridle of his faithful horse.

The young fellow's aim had been true, and the size of the wound in the man's abdomen was clear evidence of the kind of weapon that had done the dread work—a Colt revolver of the very same calibre as the one in the hands of T. N. Russell.

The body was brought back to town, and the four desperadoes, after having lain for a couple of hours piled up promiscuously in the narrow little city jail, found common lodgment in four black-varnished coffins.

They were laid out side by side in front of the barn near which their horses had been tied. They looked very ghastly and unheroic.

Here they were photographed, and from these photographs have our sketches been drawn.

There were hundreds of morbid ones who came to gaze and stayed long.

Some handled the bodies in the coffins, and whenever Grat Dalton's right arm was lifted a little spurt of blood would jump from the round black hole in his throat.

So they remained all night, and the morning

13

dust lifted by the feet of crowding bystanders
settled thickly on the corpses and open coffins.
Myriads of flies, called out by the warmth of the
sun and the smell of blood, gathered on the living
and the dead, but the crowd took no heed of the
time until noon, when there came an undertaker
who closed the coffin lids.

Early that afternoon the bodies of the robbers
were given burial, and although the Dalton family
own a lot in the cemetery there, they were buried,
two coffins in a grave, in the potter's field, within a
stone's throw of the grave of poor Charley Montgomery, the first of the victims of their murderous
guns.

Shortly after his surrender, Emmet Dalton had
been removed to a barely furnished room over Slos-
sin's drug store. There was much talk of lynching
and Sheriff Callahan, of Montgomery county, who
had arrived at once from Independence, the county
seat, was watchful during all the night.

Once there was even a pretense of an attempt at
action, but, let it be said to Coffeyville's great honor,
it came to naught. Still, during the first days of
intense excitement, any move on the part of the
sheriff to have the wounded desperado transported

THE CROWD IN FRONT OF THE COFFEYVILLE JAIL, WHERE THE BODIES OF THE FOUR DEAD BANDITS LAY.

out of the city's jurisdiction would have been stubbornly met with determined resistance. What saved the boy's life, however, was the well-substantiated rumor that he had but a few hours to live; and in fact, the doctors' verdict was that Emmet's chances of surviving were about five to a hundred against.

In spite of his terrible exhaustion and loss of blood, Emmet had already made some rambling kind of a confession, very contradictory in its details. He denied his participation in any other affairs, but admitted that Bob, Grat and their two lesser associates were in the robbery of the Missouri, Kansas & Texas train at Adair, in the robberies of the Santa Fe trains at Wharton and Red Rock, and in the California robbery. At first, he tried to deny his identity and said that his name was Bailey, but so many came who knew him that he abandoned it. Those of the desperadoes who had been killed were brought before him and he identified rightly, his two brothers, but said that Dick Broadwell was Texas Jack and that Bill Powers was Tom Evans, alias Tom Hedde. Afterward he admitted that he had lied, and the identity of every member of the gang was fully established. Others disputed Grat Dalton's identity, but there now re-

mains no question but that the outlaw is one of the dead.

Emmet Dalton passed this first night in continuous pain. Amputation of his arm was suggested, but he would not consent. At noon of the next day, he was removed to the Farmers' Home, the little frame boarding-house the Dalton brothers used to patronize on their nightly excursions, and there he lay in the front room of the smaller building, for the next five days, exposed to the gaze of hundreds.

It was there that Ransom Payne visited him on the following Saturday.

He found the wounded lad surrounded by his aged mother, wrinkled and bowed down beyond her years by unspeakable sorrow, and her eyes dim with continuous crying; by his sister, Mrs. Whipple, a comely young woman, with dark energetic features; by honest Ben Dalton, the type of the sturdy farmer of those parts, and finally by Will, the whilom Californian, suspected of, but finally acquitted from, guilty participation in the Tulare county hold-up.

As soon as Emmet, who had by this time surprisingly rallied and showed undoubted signs of recovery, saw the stalwart form of Payne approach his

bed, he stretched his hand, which the officer kindly pressed, and cried:

"So you have got us in, after all!"

Then, feeling that he could talk freely in the presence of a man who knew so thoroughly every detail of his criminal career, he made the following statement, which has certainly the appearance of ungarbled truth. He said:

"On the first of Oct., 1892, I met the boys south of Tulsa, and they asked me how much money I had. I told them about $20. I asked them how much they had, and they said about $900. I asked them what they were going to do and they said this town, Coffeyville, had been talking about them, and some of the people had been trying to get them captured. I told them I knew it was a lie, that they used to have lots of friends here.

"Bob said he could discount the James boys' work and go up and rob both banks at Coffeyville in one day.

"I told him I did not want any of it at all. He said I had better go along and help and get some money and leave the country; that if I stayed around here I was sure to get caught or killed.

"On the morning of Oct. 3rd we saddled up north

of Tulsa in the Osage nation and rode about twenty
miles toward Coffeyville, and we talked it over that
day.   I tried to prevail on the boys not to come up,
for the people here had done us no harm.   They
said all right, if I didn't want to come that they four
would come and give the town a round up.   I told
them if that was the case I might as well come with
them.   I came for the love of my brothers, and I
knew that I would be chased just as hard if I didn't
come as I would be if I did, and I had no money to
get out of the country on.

"We camped in the timbered hills on the head
of Hickory creek, about twelve miles from Coffeyville, on the night of the 4th, and in the night we
saddled up and rode to the Davis farm in the Onion
creek bottoms, and this morning (the 5th) we fed
our horses some corn.   I asked them if they were
still coming up here.   They said they were.   I told
them it would not be treating the people right, as
they had always befriended us.

"I asked them how they were going to do it.
Bob said that we would ride in about half past nine
o'clock in the morning, saying that there would not
be so many people in town to hold up, and he
wouldn't have to hurt any one.

"He told me he would like to have me go with him, because I was quick on foot, and that he and I would go to the First National bank, and let the others go to C. M. Condon's. He said we would ride in and hitch at the old C. M. Condon building. He said we would hitch there so that people would not see us until we got right into the banks.

"When we got to the lumber yard we saw that the street was all torn up, and he said: 'Let us ride down in the alley and hitch.'

"All the five horses belonged to Bob. He bought one on the 2d, and others next morning. I am a first cousin of Bob and Cole Younger. My mother is a sister of Cole Younger's father."

Later in the day, Ransom Payne had a long talk with Ben Dalton, who showed no hesitancy in expressing himself concerning his brothers. He spoke somewhat in this wise:

"I was sick in bed at our home on the farm, four miles north of Kingfisher, when we received the news of this awful affair, but managed to come with mother and the others. We had not seen the boys for a long time, and I had no idea where they were or what they were doing. I never had much in common with the ones who lie here dead and badly

EMMET DALTON LYING IN HIS ROOM IN THE FARMERS' HOME.

wounded, as I am a farmer and try to be a good citizen. I wish you would state that mother and I have no ill feeling against the people of Coffeyville and no words of censure. They simply did their duty, and while we naturally deplore the loss of our boys, we also sorrow for the citizens who gave up their lives in defense of the town. Emmet tells me he has been treated better than he hoped for by your people, and we are feeling sad but not angry."

On that same afternoon, George Broadwell, of Hutchinson, a brother of Dick Broadwell, one of the dead outlaws, and E. B. Wilcox, the bandit's brother-in-law, arrived from Hutchinson. Mr. Broadwell is a salesman for the Boston Tea Company of Chicago, while Mr. Wilcox is a grocer in Hutchinson. Mr. Wilcox said of the dead man:

"We were as greatly shocked by this occurrence as you, and entirely ignorant of Dick's being with this gang. Had not heard of him since May. He was never wild or a drinker or gambler, and although a cowboy, we always thought him to be straight and law abiding. His mother and sister Jennie, George and my wife compose the family, and all live in Hutchinson."

The grave containing the coffins of Broadwell and Powers was opened and Broadwell's coffin taken out.

The body was then clad in a new suit of clothing, placed in an expensive coffin and reinterred. It was thought at the time that the bodies of the other bandits ought to be exhumed and a careful examination made of their clothing, as there might have been money or valuables sewn in the lining of the garments, but the idea was not acted upon.

Mr. Broadwell endeavored to obtain his brother's horse, which had been neither killed nor wounded, and the $92.40 found on his person, but those who held the property refused to turn it over, although an indemnifying bond was offered. None of the friends of Bill Powers, alias Tom Evans, put in an appearance, nor have they been heard from.

The body of Lucius M. Baldwin, the first victim of the outlaws and a most worthy young man, was shipped to his mother at Burlington, Kan., on the following morning. George Cubine was buried that same afternoon, and all the stores of the town were closed and draped in black. The funeral was very large and most impressive in its simplicity. Mr. Cubine was a member of the M. E. church.

The Missouri Pacific Railway Company kindly furnished two coaches, free of charge, and placed them at the disposal of the family and friends of

the dead Marshal Connelly, for the purpose of con-
veying them to Independence, where the funeral
occurred on Friday.

Charles T. Connelly, the dead hero, was born in
the state of Indiana, November 25, 1845, where he
resided until he moved to Kansas in 1885. He enlisted in the Ninth Indiana Battery at the age of
seventeen years and served his country gallantly
until the close of the war. In the year 1867 he was
married to Mary McCord. Two children, Bert and
Grace, blessed their union. His wife died in 1874.
Two years after her death he was married to Sarah
Alexander. This union was also blessed with two
children, but one of whom is living, Miss Jessie. As
a teacher in Coffeyville city schools, Mr. Connelly
was ever faithful and efficient, and enjoyed the con-
fidence and esteem of his pupils. As city marshal
he discharged his duty with great courage and absolute fidelity to the best interests of the city. He
gave his life freely in defense of the lives and
property of the citizens, and his faithfulness to duty
will ever be held in grateful remembrance by the
people of Coffeyville. The deepest sympathy of
the entire community and the people at large went
out to the bereaved wife and children as they

mourned the loss of a loving and devoted husband and father.

The remains of the courageous old shoemaker, Charles Brown, were sent to Harley, S. D., where his wife resides.

All the wounded citizens, including Cashier Ayers, who was thought to have been fatally shot by Bob Dalton's unerring Winchester, have recovered from their injuries.

Finally, at a very early hour on the Tuesday following the great tragedy—the 11th of October it was—Emmet Dalton was taken to Independence to jail by Sheriff Callahan, without any objection by the citizens. William went along. Now that all the Dalton crowd had gone the citizens felt relieved, as their presence kept the town full of undesirable visitors who were apt to cause trouble. It was thought then that Emmet would recover, and so he did.

With his capture and the certainty of his being sent to the penitentiary for life (since the death penalty is never enforced in the state of Kansas), the Dalton gang is practically annihilated, and whatever remains of it is deprived of the bold and intelligent leadership of Bob, so strongly backed by the devotion and reckless intrepidity of his brothers.

For a while—for a long while, we hope the territories and border states are to be freed from the constant terror which the Dalton gang had contrived to spread through this prosperous country.

Ransom Payne had not toiled in vain.

Driven to extraordinarily desperate acts of criminality in their anxiety to obtain resources enough to flee the vicinity, the Dalton boys and their pals had run head foremost into the jaws of death

CHAPTER VI.

THE SCATTERED REMNANTS OF THE DALTON GANG
THREATEN DIRE REVENGE–"THE WHOLE CROWD AIN'T
DEAD, BY A—SIGHT!"—HEROIC JOHN KLOEHR RE-
CEIVES A "SKULL AND CROSS-BONES" WARNING—
THE COFFEYVILLE PEOPLE READY FOR THEM—
UNIVERSAL SYMPATHY FOR THE VICTIMS AND
THE INTREPID DEFENDERS OF THE LAW—
THE BANKERS ALL OVER THE COUNTRY
SUBSCRIBE LARGE SUMS–THE R. R. COM-
PANIES URGED TO PAY THE RE-
WARDS–A GOLD MEDAL PRESENT-
ED TO JOHN J. KLOEHR BY HIS
CHICAGO ADMIRERS–A TRAGE-
DY NOT SOON TO BE
FORGOTTEN.

A week had hardly elapsed after the terrible events of the 5th of October, 1892, had taken place, than an alarming rumor gained ground all over Southwestern Kansas.

"The Dalton gang had not been wholly extermi-
nated; the survivors were coming on to wreck their
vengeance upon valiant Coffeyville!"

The report started from the robbing of the Missouri
Pacific train at near Caney, a small place a few miles
from Coffeyville, during the night of October 13th.

Just as the train drew up at Caney at 10:15
o'clock that night, two masked men, heavily armed,
climbed on the locomotive tender from the front
of the combination baggage and express car and
covered Engineer Eggleston and his fireman with
their rifles.

The locomotive engineer was ordered to pull
slowly to the switch, where there was no danger of
molestation.

At the whistling post the outlaws ordered the
engineer to stop and made the fireman uncouple
the express car from the rest of the train. This was
done so quietly that no one in the coaches was disturbed.

The engineer then pulled ahead with the express
car. When a deep-cut half a mile farther on was
reached the engine was halted.

Express Messenger J. N. Maxwell, who had witnessed the uncoupling, had in the meantime blown

out his lights and barred and barricaded the doors.

The order to open the car elicited no response, and the robbers began firing into the sides of the car.

Maxwell answered the shots with his revolvers for a few minutes, but finally received a bullet in his right arm, which disabled him. The robbers ordered him to light his lamps and open the car door, and as soon as he had done so they entered the car, with the engineer in front of them as a shield. Maxwell was then forced to open his safe and deliver his watch and personal property. The men backed off the car and disappeared in the darkness.

Messenger Maxwell declares that the robbers secured less than $100 all told. The men engaged in that night's work were thought immediately to be those pals of the Daltons who had not reached Coffeyville in time to take part in the tragic raid on the fifth.

It was understood to be sufficient evidence that the gang was being rapidly reorganized and was moving upon Coffeyville with the avowed purpose of avenging the death of their pals.

Couriers arrived in Coffeyville at an early hour

14

the next morning, bearing this important news, the word was passed around, and in the shortest possible time the people were armed and ready to defend their homes against the invasion of the threatened mob. Since the Dalton massacre many persons have been noticed in Coffeyville, openly condemning the manner in which this notorious gang met its death, and several sympathizers have even been arrested and confined in jail.

All of the rifles in the town were in readiness, and every man stood waiting for an attack. A car from the M., K. & T., at Parsons, stood at the depot barricaded and armed.

In the Coffeyville homes, women and children were frightened over the outlook for another bloody encounter with the bandits. Still, the mayor of Coffeyville, after having conferred with the railroad officials, wired to Parsons that the people here could care for themselves, as the number of the attacking party was greatly magnified, and that a matter of a few hours would result in their capture.

"Coffeyville people," said he, " have shown their ability to care for themselves."

Ben and William Dalton, and many of their sympathizers, had been loitering about Coffeyville for

days. When Emmet Dalton's wounded body was removed to Independence, Ben and William and their mother accompanied him. Since then nothing had been heard from them. That evening a bonfire was started on the plaza of the town to furnish a reassuring illumination.

The information of the approach of the Daltons had been conveyed to the people of Coffeyville by the force under Detective Dodge, of the Wells-Fargo Company, who is scouring the Indian Territory for members of the gang.

One of his men heard it and wired the mayor of Coffeyville, who asked for help from Parsons and had it kept there in readiness. The plan was for one of the surviving Daltons and forty whites and half-breeds, completely armed, to ride into Coffeyville at 9 o'clock on that night and wipe out the place. No mercy was to be given, according to Dodge's information.

Since then, of course, the town of Coffeyville has been a pandemonium of excitement, yet no braver set of men ever shouldered a gun than the gallant and fearless citizens of this little Kansas town.

There is every reason to believe from the actions of some of the men who have visited Coffeyville

that if Emmet Dalton recovers, some steps will be taken by his friends to liberate him. The people of Coffeyville will see to it that he gets his just deserts, even if they again have to resort to arms.

The following letter, received by John Kloehr, the man who is most justly credited with having killed three out of four of the Dalton gang, shows at least that all of the gang is not dead:

"ARKANSAS CITY, Kas., Oct. —, 1892. To John Kloehr—Dear Sir: I take the time to tell you and the citizens of Coffeyville that all of the gang ain't dead yet by a —— of a sight, and don't you forget it. I would have given all I ever made to have been there the 5th. There are five of the gang left, and we shall come and see you all some day. That day, Oct. 5, we were down in the Chickasaw Nation, and we did not know it was coming off so soon. We thought it was to be Nov. 5. We shall have revenge for your killing of Bob and Grat and the rest of them. You people had no cause to take arms against the gang. The bankers will not help the widows of the men that got killed there, and you thought you were playing —— when you killed three of us, but your time will soon come, when you will have to go into the grave and pass in your checks for the killing of

Bob and Joe Evans and Texas Jack, so take warning. We will leave you in the hands of God for this time. Yours truly, DALTON GANG

"And sympathizer of this gang of outlaws."

This letter, which bears new testimony to the great courage displayed by John Kloehr in thus jeopardizing his life, not only in the fight but for a long time after, renders doubly opportune the token of high esteem presented to this brave man by bankers and citizens of the city of Chicago.

The First National Bank of the western metropolis, aided by contributions from nearly all the banks in that city, ordered an elegant badge, which was recently placed on exhibition at Chamber & Co.'s store. It has since been sent by express to the courageous defender of Coffeyville.

A semi-circular plate of gold bears the name of "John Joseph Kloehr." Below this is a gold ribbon on which is engraved: "The Emergency Arose. The Man Appeared." Suspended from this by three gold links at each end is the badge proper, a gold circle two and one-fourth inches in diameter, with a narrow raised band on the outer edge. Next within this is an open scroll-work, then another raised band of bright gold, and within this a laurel wreath. A

third raised band of bright gold incloses an eight-pointed bright gold star, in the center of which is a large diamond, the star being three-quarters of an inch in diameter.

Badge presented to John J. Kloehr by the Banks of Chicago.

The entire badge is four inches in length and cost $350. On the reverse is the inscription: "Presented by friends in Chicago, who admire nerve and courage when displayed in defense of social order."

We give herein an exact reproduction of this beautiful badge.

Neither have the families of the victims of Bob

Dalton's and his pals' Winchesters been forgotten either in their own city or through the country at large.

A mass meeting of the citizens of Coffeyville was held on the Friday following the tragedy, for the purpose of taking action in respect to the matter of aid for the families of the men who died in defense of the property of their fellow-citizens, or were wounded in the fight with the Dalton gang on the Wednesday preceding.

Thomas Scurr, Jr., president of the First National bank, presided, and D. Stewart Elliott, editor of *The Journal*, a most excellent weekly paper that does the greatest honor to its editor and publisher, was made secretary. It was resolved to immediately prepare and send out an appeal circular to the banks, monetary institutions, railroad and express companies, asking contributions for the purpose above stated.

The following committee of prominent business men was appointed to issue the circular: Charles T. Carpenter, Dr. T. C. Frazier, J. J. Barndollar, William McCoy and H. W. Read. The First National bank and the bank of C. M. Condon & Co. were designated as the custodians of the funds received. The committee met and organized after the adjournment

of the meeting when the paper was prepared and the following subscriptions received:

First National Bank..$000

C. M. Condon & Co...$500

The committee was directed to make weekly reports of amounts received through the city papers. C. T. Carpenter was made chairman and Dr. T. C Frazier secretary of the committee.

On the day preceding, the president of the Union National Bank of Minneapolis had already sent a message to William B. Green, Secretary of the American Bank Association in New York, asking why it would not be a good idea to call upon all members of the American Bank Association to contribute each $5 to $10 for a fund for the members of the families of the men shot down in Coffeyville, Kan., in the Dalton bank robbery raid.

His appeal was heeded, for, on October 20th, the Kansas State Bankers' Association meeting at Topeka took action regarding the fund for the slayers of the Dalton gang. This fund then reached nearly $18,000 from all sources. The Bankers' association required all members to forward their individual subscriptions and added $137. The association also organized a protective association with $2,000 in the

treasury, for the purpose of hunting down and prosecuting all persons who defraud or attempt to defraud any of its members. The sum is to be kept intact by assessments whenever rewards and prosecuting expenses have used any portion of it.

There gathered in Coffeyville during the days immediately following the tragedy from fifteen to twenty railway and express company officials. These gentlemen unanimously requested their companies to pay the full rewards to the families of the dead citizens, and all expect favorable responses to their requests.

It is to our personal knowledge that the rewards offered by the Southern Pacific R. R. Company and by the Wells, Fargo Express Company, after the Tulare county outrage, are still *alive* and will be most probably paid to those entitled to them or their heirs.

As to the reward offered by the M., K. & T. R. R., after the Adair hold-up (July 14, 1892), they have been officially withdrawn, on September 15th last.

So much about the rewards, which, in our opinion, will not be paid to any one, dead or alive, for there is no absolute evidence as to who the actual

slayers of the bandits may be, as the latter all died of many wounds. The Daltons and Bill Powers ought to be credited to Kloehr and Seaman, and Broadwell to young Russell. But it would have taken a much more thorough examination of the bodies before interment to reach the indisputable truth in the matter.

Corporations are known to be heartless. There is hardly any hope that they will show themselves different in this particular occasion.

Speaking of money, the two following items are not without some interest.

It appears that the money secured from the First National Bank amounted to $20,240 and that from Condon's $3,000.

The amounts turned over to the banks exceed this amount and serves to verify the statement by Emmet Dalton that they had $900 when they came to the town.

And, now, just as this final chapter is going to press, we hear that the surviving Daltons propose suing the city of Coffeyville for that very amount of $900, although it be, without any manner of doubt, the proceeds of some anterior and successful robbery, the Adair hold-up most probably.

Let us now close this minute record of one of the briefest but most bloody careers of crime ever heard of in modern times, and give in full the valuable opinion of Superintendent Murray concerning those gangs of train robbers who have made traveling in the Southwest much too picturesque for absolute comfort.

After praising as it behooved the valiance of the small Coffeyville community, the superintendent added:

"The Dalton gang were desperate, reckless men. They never hesitated to shoot. Their character was known all over the West. It was one thing to talk about facing them and another to do it. The Daltons did no work in the East. They seldom, in fact, got very far away from the lairs in the territory. The Coffeyville people made a clean sweep of the worst members of the gang.

"There is a certain bravado that glorifies characters such as the Daltons in the minds of tough men, and they are easily rallied around a leader bent on crimes that involve daring. The 'bad men' in the country who are liable to rob trains are narrowed down to Chris Evans and John Sontag. Under the leadership of George C. Contant, alias Sontag,

they robbed the Southern Pacific train between Visalia and Fresno, August 4th. Four people were killed in the fight which occurred. Chris Evans and John Sontag got away and are in the mountains back of Visalia. There is a reward of ten thousand dollars offered for their capture. It was this gang that committed the famous express train robbery at Western Union Junction. Their depredations have been many.

"The other celebrated train robbers are either dead or in prison. Captain Bunch, Rube Burrows, Jim Burrows, and Rube Smith are dead. The Pegleg gang in Colorado are in the penitentiary. The Cooleys, who were graduating from henroost robberies into much more serious crimes in Pennsylvania, have met with a check in the killing of one of their number.

"But none of those gangs ever equaled, in such a short space of time, the daring criminality of those four young men who are now lying stiff and stark, in their coffins, in the Potter's field by Coffeyville, Kan."

[THE END.]